Staying There

A Sanctum of Intimacy

By

Cheryl L. Wakes

ISBN: 1-4140-1525-9 (Paperback)

This book is printed on acid free paper.

1stBooks - rev. 03/19/04

DEDICATION

This book is dedicated to all those who hurt and all who minister to the hurting. It is dedicated to those who live in shame because of their past. It is my sincere desire that this book will serve in freeing you from bondage. May you come to realize God's love for you and your worth to Him.

Regardless of the position you hold in business or in ministry, regardless of your lack of biblical knowledge or aptitude, regardless of your strengths or weaknesses, there is a chapter in here for you. It is to mankind that I dedicate *STAYING THERE*.

CONTENTS

DEDICATION iii

ACKNOWLEDGMENTS vii

FOREWORD ix

INTRODUCTION xi

A GLIMPSE into "MY SANCTUM OF INTIMACY" xiii

AUTHOR'S PRAYER xix

CHAPTERS

1.   THE WATERFALL 3
The Birth 4
The Anointing 6
The Endowing 11

2.   THE WILDERNESS 17
The Outcome of Choice 23

3.   THE RAINBOW 31
The SON Makes the Difference 33
Why Warfare? 35

4.   THE PATH 41
The Journey 43

5.   THE STAR 51
A Shining Example 54

6.   THE BRIDGE 61
    A Night to Remember.. 62
    The Retreat... 65
    A Healing... 71

7.   THE BATTLEGROUND 77
    Dart Damage 79
    Choose Your Battle.. 83
    Fear versus Faith.. 86

8.   THE PORTAL 91
    Can God Get a Witness?... 93
    Just Like Jesus 97

9.   THE STORM 103
    A Firm Foundation 106

ADDENDUM - A Message From The Author 111

    THE COLORS OF CHRISTMAS............................ 113

AUTHOR'S CLOSING PRAYER 119

REFERENCES.. 121

SCRIPTURE INDEX.. 123

ACKNOWLEDGMENTS

I thank my husband for his patience during the writing of this book. His insight and wisdom are reflected throughout these pages. My Melvin is truly a godly man and a loving husband.

I am grateful to my daughter, Tracie, for being so supportive and also for allowing me to write about her. Thank you baby for not letting me give up.

I am thankful to my dad (deceased) and to my mom. I would not have endeavored to write this book had it not been for the self-esteem they instilled in me.

I wish my Nana were alive so that she could see how the treasures (her prayers) she laid up for me in heaven have brought so many blessings into my life. Thank you Nana.

I acknowledge my Heavenly Father who, through the unction of the Holy Spirit, inspired me to write this book.

I am grateful for the anointed women He has placed in my life. They have been an encouragement and a blessing to me always.

I am indebted to Denise (my Niecy) for the patience and the love she put into helping me edit this book.

And I am so very, very thankful that Jesus died for *me*. To God be the glory.

FOREWORD

STAYING THERE comes straight from the heart of God. That Cheryl Wakes is attentive to the voice of God is undeniable. That she enjoys the intimate embrace of her Father is certain. Thanks be to God that she is sharing the intimacy of their relationship with us.

STAYING THERE is an experience of hope. *STAYING THERE* demands that we have the courage to wait on the Lord until His purpose in every experience is realized. Wakes launches each chapter with a Holy Spirit inspired image. Hope being implanted within each of them. The images are alive and vivid. They are provocative and compelling. Each one draws us into a place of wonder, and blessed contemplation. Every sense is employed. Wherever we look in nature, within ourselves, in the things our hands have fashioned—we find a message from God.

STAYING THERE challenges us. Who can resist the temptation to stay underneath a *waterfall* of His anointing, feeling the oil as it saturates, sanctifying us entirely—body, soul, and spirit. The *wilderness* calls us to remember that in spite of the desolation we may see with our eyes, God is still at work refining us. The ancient promise of the *rainbow* becomes a visual reminder of eternal hope and ushers us into unbridled praise, and adoring worship. The *path* with its signposts, twists, turns, and fellow travelers leads us to a place of union with God. Then there is the *star*, the *bridge*, the *battleground,* and the *portal*—each one taking us into a transformational encounter. Feel the sure grip of His hand on yours securing you in the rage of the *storm*s of life. Finally, never again will you be able to gaze upon the *colors of Christmas* without being immediately transported to the Cross.

You must read each chapter devotionally. This book is to be read slowly and purposefully. You will want to devour it in one sitting. Resist the temptation. Savor each morsel. Read it with pen, and paper prepared to record whatever God chooses to speak to your heart. Stay there! He will surely meet you on the pages of this love gift. As you begin, ask the Holy Spirit to reveal to you truths about yourself, others, and God. Consider how God would have you to respond to your newfound knowledge. Be prepared to be obedient. Stay there until He releases you. Then praise the AWESOME GOD.

Patricia F. Foote, Pastor
Grace Church
Cleveland Heights, Ohio

INTRODUCTION

I have often found that for one to be effective spiritually in another person's life, one must sometimes expose one's own heart and soul. In *STAYING THERE,* I have not only done that, but I have revealed to the reader my weaknesses and shortcomings, as well as my love and heartfelt hunger for God.

There are nine short narratives within these pages, six being the number of man and three being the number of divinity. The divine Creator—God desires fellowship with His creation—man.

STAYING THERE is a devotional book although it is different from a daily devotional. However, like a daily devotional, it too is designed to encourage you to live a life that is devoted to God.

STAYING THERE depicts the who, the where, the when, and the why. Often we speak of seeing the evidence of God in nature, but how often do we equate the evidence of His existence to our daily lives? When you see a star do you think of your relationship to the Heavenly Father? When you see a bridge do you think about how Jesus bridged the gap between you and the Father?

Jesus says, "There is no way to the Father but by me." Are you secure enough in your relationship with God to feel comfortable with other saints? If you find that in some way you feel inferior in the presence of other believers, you may need to check your relationship with God. On the other hand if you feel superior to other saints, you may need to check your relationship with God. *STAYING THERE will* help you to do that.

When you wander into a dry place have you found yourself feeling desolate and afraid? What or who is your focus when you are going through a wilderness experience? Is it on you, your circumstances, or is it on God?

My prayer is that *STAYING THERE* will encourage you to stay in the presence of God so that you will fully complete His will for your life. No matter what direction your life may take, remember *The Waterfall* and *The Path.* Don't just reach for the stars, *be* a star.

Your solution to whatever you are going through is well within your grasp.

Now sit back, take a deep breath and relax. Enjoy a cup of tea, or coffee, or a glass of lemonade as I speak to you from the pages of this book. God bless you as you read.

A glimpse into *"My Sanctum of Intimacy"*

...I've finished reading Brother Lawrence. I am sleepy now. I desire to lie down, close my eyes, and commune with the Lord upon my bed, just as David did. I pray that God will bless my dreams with thoughts and visions of Himself.

...Lord give me the strength to open myself up for whatever you have for me, no matter what it may be. I don't want to be afraid of the cost.

...All I can think about right now is how much liberty I have in Jesus. I have the freedom to call His name and cry out to Him whenever I want. I have the freedom to praise Him. I have the freedom to tell Him my most intimate feelings. I don't have to be ashamed or embarrassed before Him, because nothing is hidden from Him and he loves me better than I love myself. I am free to weep in his presence. He stores my tears in a sacred place, for they are the tears of joy as I remember and remember. Oh how you have loved me Lord. I have failed you so many times and you have loved me much, so very much. Thank you.

God I am so thankful for Jesus and the salvation I have received through Him. You have truly blessed me with the fellowship of your Holy Spirit. I'm so grateful that you desire me to worship you and you are bringing me into the knowledge of how to worship you effortlessly. How blessed I am that you have that kind of love and consideration for me.

...I opened my bible and read these verses:

Luke 7:36-48

And one of the Pharisees desired him that he would eat with him. And he went into the Pharisee's house, and sat down to meat. And, behold, a woman in the city, which was a sinner, when she knew that Jesus sat at meat in the Pharisee's house, brought an alabaster box of ointment. And stood at his feet behind him weeping, and began to wash his feet with tears, and did wipe them with the hairs of her head, and kissed his feet, and anointed them with the ointment. Now when the Pharisee which had bidden him saw it, he spake within himself, saying, This man, if he were a prophet, would have known who and what manner of woman this is that toucheth him: for she is a sinner. And Jesus answering said unto him, Simon, I have somewhat to say unto thee. And he saith, Master, say on.

There was a certain creditor which had two debtors: the one owed five hundred pence, and the other fifty. And when they had nothing to pay, he frankly forgave them both. Tell me therefore, which of them will love him most? Simon answered and said, I suppose that he, to whom he forgave most. And he said unto him, Thou hast rightly judged. And he turned to the woman, and said unto Simon, Seest thou this woman? I entered into thine house, thou gavest me no water for my feet: but she hath washed my feet with tears, and wiped them with the hairs of her head. Thou gavest me no kiss: but this woman since the time I came in hath not ceased to kiss my feet. My head with oil thou didst not anoint: but this woman hath anointed my feet with ointment. Wherefore I say unto thee, Her sins, which are many, are forgiven; for she loved much: but to whom little is forgiven, the same loveth little. And he said unto her, Thy sins are forgiven.

When I finished reading I wrote this short poem:

To whom much is forgiven, much should be required.

To whom much love is shown, much should be their desire.

To please the Lord with all their heart, for giving them a brand new start.

To whom much love is given, much should be required.

...There is none like you Father God; you bring me such beautiful thoughts. Thank you. I love you God. Each time I am in your presence, I feel like a woman who has met a new love and I want to please him.

...Yesterday my Father gave me a vision of something that I will try to put into writing. Sometimes we see ourselves as big fat zeroes. If we lift a zero off of a page, we would grab it at the top and peel it off. God does not pull us up by our hair or grab us by the collar.

He can get between the paper and the zero. He can scoop the zero off the paper. Lovingly He scoops us up, therefore filling in the zero with the fullness of Himself. When the zero is filled in, it becomes a symbol of wholeness and solidarity. Thank you, my Father, for all the times you gently scooped me up. I bless your name.

...Yesterday I didn't write in my journal. Today as I read the 19th division of Psalm, which David wrote to his chief musician, I could see him giving the words to his Musician and telling him to put some beautiful music to it. I am so grateful to God for the way He quickens His word in me.

...As I began to pray this morning, all the cares and the worries of the day began to flood my mind [as if I know what the day will bring]. But Jesus, being larger than the sum of them all, interceded and ushered me into the presence of His Father. I was reminded to pray for the defeat of the princes of the air over our cities, as they attempt to fulfill their assignments. This day, I pray the host of heaven will come against every assignment of the evil one. I am so grateful for the authority and the privilege given to me because of the blood of Jesus.

(This part of my journal was written while on a retreat)

...I left the porch and walked down to that large body of water, thinking how frightening the water was to me. And God said, "When you see me in things, you don't have to be frightened."

...God does not want to use satan to arouse us out of a state of apathy, but He will. He would rather have us respond to Him, when He speaks [so we must listen].

...Going through a trial is like fasting. We can do it because it is only temporary and we know it will be over soon. Weeping may endure for a night, but joy comes in the morning.

God wants us to take one step at a time and make sure that step is forward. We will be walking toward a future with eternity with God and He is going to receive our report on how well we abstained from the world and ate only what was prepared at His table.

These are only a few excerpts from the author's journal. These reveal communion between the author and her Father.

The LORD desires the same communion from us all. How does your journal read?

AUTHOR'S PRAYER

My Heavenly Father, how excellent are your names in all the earth. I give you praise and honor and glory.

Father, it is my sincere desire to honor you with my life. It is you, Father, who gave me life. It is you who has made eternal life available to me by the gift of your Son. I am so grateful and I thank you with all my heart. Father, I exalt you by sharing your presence in my life with others.

As you have charged me to make my home a portal to your Kingdom, I pray that others will also embrace that charge. Father, I thank you for presence of mind and a heartfelt desire to serve you.

I pray for a special anointing on all who read this book. I pray that their hunger for You will never end. I ask that You would give them new revelation.

I pray they will come to know a part of You, which they have never before experienced. I pray as they read, there will be a decrease in their flesh, and an increase in their spirit.

Bless them Father, that they may know you are a loving father, a father who is willing to protect and comfort. All these things I ask in Jesus' name. Amen.

THE WATERFALL

THE WATERFALL

Imagine standing under a waterfall. But instead of water, it's a thin shimmering sheet of oil. Don't be appalled. It's not cooking oil, it's not even olive oil. It's the oil of the Holy Spirit. As you stand under the waterfall, God is anointing you. Your spirit is being revived as the oil cascades over your entire being. Sense the presence of God as He saturates you and equips you for service. Feel the Holy Spirit empowering you for what lies ahead. Begin to pray. Pour your heart out to God. Close your eyes and enjoy His essence. Take a few moments, but don't fall asleep.

Was it difficult for you to open your eyes and face the present? I know it was for me. Did you merely close your eyes and open them again, wondering what you were supposed to feel? Unsure of what should have happened? Do you believe there is an anointing that comes from God? Did you know that all believers are anointed?

The anointing will give you the awareness of being in the presence of the Lord. If experiencing the presence of God is not a daily occurrence, I pray this book will awaken in you a desire to seek God in every area of your life. I pray He will be a conscious part of your daily decision-making.

3

To be anointed means to be sanctified by God for your assigned task. It is the process by which God prepares you. It is personal and it is spiritual.

God desires a personal relationship with each and every one of us. God is bigger than life for He holds all life within Himself. His love for us has no boundaries. Over and over in the following chapters I will make reference to "intimacy." I have come to realize that many Christians lack a genuinely intimate relationship with God. God wants us to seek Him. He wants us to know Him. He wants intimacy.

The LORD looks down from heaven upon the children of men to see if there are any that act wisely, that seek after God (Psalm 14:2).

The lack of an intimate relationship with our Heavenly Father can result in confusion, indecisiveness, fear, failure, and loneliness. But I will speak more on those things in the following chapters. If you are having difficulty maintaining intimacy with the Lord the chapter on *The Path* will be of help to you.

THE BIRTH

STAYING THERE was born one day as I was working out on my treadmill. It was a cool May morning; I arose and went about the morning ritual of brushing my teeth and washing my face. I then returned to my bedroom to pray. Routinely after prayer I would dress and go downstairs.

This particular morning however, I donned a sweat suit. I had vowed to take better care of my temple (body), so I geared up in preparation of hitting the treadmill, something I had not done in two years. Feeling as if I had already carried out my duty (prayer) so to speak, my plan was to watch television while I ran in place.

Before I go any further let me clarify something. Prayer is not a duty in respect to a task, but it is our duty, as Christians, in respect to a charge given by God.

The word of God says, *And he spake a parable unto them to this end, that men ought always to pray, and not to faint (Luke 18:1).*

I headed toward the stairs leading to my third floor where the treadmill was located. As I climbed the stairs, the scripture in 1 Thessalonians 5:17, *Pray without ceasing,* came into my mind. Suddenly I heard the Lord say, "Don't turn on the television."

In obedience (something I should put into practice more often) I left the television off.

Not being one who gets into exercising, I regarded my time on the treadmill as a real drag. Drag or not, it was a necessary means to an end—the end of an overweight body.

Running in place on a treadmill can be very monotonous. In order to make the time go faster, since I didn't have the television set on, I closed my eyes and began to pray. There's always so much to pray about, occasionally my prayer time would exceed an hour.

As I prayed for God's anointing on the five-fold ministry, a waterfall came into my view. God began to reveal to me the progression of the anointing. He expressed the importance of *staying there*.

"Where is *there?*" You might ask. *There* is the place where God tells you to meet Him. *There* is the place where He tells you to go and be fed. *There* is the place where He has told you to minister. *There* is anywhere God instructs you to be. He has already given you above all you can think or ask. You already have the staying power within you; you need only to go *there* and wait.

THE ANOINTING

As you stand under the waterfall of God's anointing you become drenched. Yet there are some who will quickly pass through the waterfall. Those are the ones who are satisfied with only receiving a splash of the anointing. They are satisfied with just enough to feel that they are of some use to God. Mighty works are not that important to them.

Those receiving a "splash" will begin to dry up much quicker than the person who has been drenched. The longer you *stay there* the more you will absorb. The more you absorb the longer it stays with you. You will do "greater works" for the kingdom of God.

People who are satisfied with just enough of the anointing to appear "spiritual" have nothing to spread on others. On the other hand, those that have spent time in the presence of God do. They have been saturated and you will sense the presence of God when they enter a room. You will be blessed just by being in their company. Or you may be the one blessing others because *you* stayed there.

Have you ever been around a person whose very presence makes you feel safe and comfortable?

You begin to share things that you had no intention of speaking aloud. It was the anointing on them that made you feel you could trust them. Or possibly the Holy Spirit caused someone to open up to you merely because you were in the right place at the right time and functioning under His direction. *Staying there* is not always easy. In fact, it is very difficult at first.

After a while I wanted to get off of the treadmill.

God said, "*Stay there,* I'm not through. Consider what you want to accomplish."

I began to envision my physical body without fat, but what about the spiritual part of me? What about the intemperance in my spirit? There were things there I needed to shed also.

God said, "One day at a time, s*tay there.*"

Running in place with my eyes closed, I began to notice the beautiful landscape that surrounded the waterfall. The waterfall was located in a valley. The valley was sun-drenched. The scenery was lush. The grass that ran up the sides of the hills was tall, and green, and even. A cave had been carved out of the side of one hill. The waterfall flowed out from that hill as if some huge invisible faucet

7

atop it had been turned on. The thin sheet of oil shimmered as it flowed down over the mouth of the cave. Inside the cave, rather than being made of dirt, the walls appeared to be made of stone. Although the origin of the flowing oil was invisible, the flow was continuous.

Directly in front of the waterfall thousands of rocks formed a path, which seemed to lead deep into the valley. The oil cascaded downward causing the rocks to glisten in the brightness of the sun. There were no visible clouds, only the softness of the blue sky. Except for the flowing of the oil, all was tranquil.

I sat behind the flow in the grotto, looking out through the glistening oil at all the beauty God had created. The rich green grass, the soft blue sky, and the marbleized rocks. A colorful flower had been added here and there as if for effect. In concert they formed a finished picture painted by an exceptionally skilled artist. Suddenly I had no problem *staying there.* It was pleasing and peaceful. I sighed as I thought, surely this was the blessing of being in the presence of God, this fulfillment of peace.

But after surveying my surroundings, I knew that my departure from the grotto would have to be supernatural. The only way out was the path directly in front leading down, deep into the valley.

As much as I wanted to stay there, I could not. I was on a treadmill and at some point I had to open my eyes and face what was real.

Although God and the things of God are eternal, in reality the world today does not offer beauty, peace, or serenity. Instead it is filled with much chaos, misery, and pain.

I brought the treadmill to a halt. Stepping off, I hurried downstairs to take off the wet clothing. I was anxious to capture on paper what I had experienced and here I sit at my computer slowly pecking away.

As I pondered on *staying there,* many Biblical characters came to mind. I am reminded of the sequence of events concerning Elijah. God told Elijah, the Tishbite, to get away from Gilead. The Bible states, *then the word of the LORD came to him, saying, "Get away from here and turn eastward, and hide by the Brook Cherith, which flows into the Jordan. And it will be that you shall drink from the brook, and I have commanded the ravens to feed you there."*

So he went and did according to the word of the LORD, for he went and stayed by the Brook Cherith, which flows into the Jordan. The ravens brought him bread and meat in the morning, and bread and meat in the evening; and he drank from the brook.

After the brook dried up the LORD told Elijah, Arise, go to Zarephath, which belongs to Sidon, and dwell there. See, I have commanded a widow there to provide for you. So he arose and went to Zarephath. And when he came to the gate of the city, indeed a widow was there gathering sticks. And he called to her and said, please bring me a little water in a cup, that I may drink (1 Kings 17:2-10).

Elijah was fed. He was in the place where the Lord directed him to go and he stayed. When the water in that place dried up, the Lord told him where to go to quench his thirst.

There is the place you will be fed. *There* is the place your thirst for God's word will be fulfilled. And your hunger for His presence will be satisfied.

I wondered why I pictured myself merely sitting in the grotto behind the flowing oil. Why wasn't I under it being saturated with the anointing? Then I remembered another episode of Elijah's life.

The widow had a son who became ill and died. The Bible tells it like this. *Now it happened after these things that the son of the woman who owned the house became sick. And his sickness was so serious that there was no breath left in him* [in other words he died].

So she (the widow) said to Elijah, "What have I to do with you, O man of God?

Have you come to me to bring my sin to remembrance, and to kill my son?"

And he said to her, "Give me your son."

So he took him out of her arms and carried him to the upper room where he was staying, and laid him on his own bed. Then he cried out to the LORD and said, "O LORD my God, have you also brought tragedy on the widow with whom I lodge, by killing her son?"

And he stretched himself out on the child three times, and cried out to the LORD and said, "O LORD my God, I pray, let this child's soul come back to him."

Then the LORD heard the voice of Elijah; and the soul of the child came back to him, and he revived. And Elijah took the child and brought him down from the upper room into the house, and gave him to his mother. And Elijah said, "See, your son lives!"

Then the woman said to Elijah, "Now by this I know that you are a man of God, and that the word of the LORD in your mouth is the truth" (1 Kings 17:17-24).

Elijah had gone where God told him to go, he stayed as long as God told him to stay, and he did what God told him to do. Now he was prepared to be of service to God on behalf of this poor widow woman. The anointing was on him so heavily he brought a dead child back to life.

Sitting behind the waterfall was my time and place of preparation. Once I stood under it the next step would be to move out. Go. Be ready for whatever the Lord instructed me to do.

I bowed my head and prayed, "Lord prepare me, empower me, strengthen me, and sanctify me that I may be equipped to serve you." I stood up and walked toward the cascading oil.

THE ENDOWING

The waterfall characterizes the application of oil, and the oil symbolizes authority and power.

God anointed Jesus of Nazareth with the Holy Spirit and with power (Acts 10:38).

Stay under the waterfall a few moments longer as you allow the Spirit of God to refresh you with the oil of His anointing. While you are there use the time to search your heart. Ask God to show you yourself in the light of His glory. Sometimes there are things in us that need to be addressed before we can be a blessing to someone else.

Biblically the oil had many purposes. It was used on dead bodies to check decay. Is there anything rotting in your spirit that would interfere with your assignment? Every Christian has an assignment. Begin right now and rid yourself of the things which are bringing death to your spirit. Excessive sorrow, heartbreak, and being overly anxious will grieve your spirit.

The oil was also used for healing. When there is unforgiveness, or feelings of animosity in your heart, there is a need for healing. God wants to apply the healing oil to your heart. Events occur which may make you angry with God. You need to get beyond that if you don't want your prayers to be hindered.

Experience the waterfall. Feel the oil massaging your heart. Softening it and making you ready. Allow God to do a work in you. You are valuable to Him.

Oil was also used in the making of perfumes. The most expensive perfumes contain rare flower oils. Though some may find the fragrances of jasmine, orange blossom, and rose to be a heavenly aroma, they cannot compare to the sweet fragrance experienced while in the presence of God.

Close your eyes again and remain under the flowing oil a bit longer. Wait for your assignment. Wait for your healing. Wait for your deliverance. Wait for Him to empower you. ENJOY THE INTIMACY.

While you are waiting think on, *Whatever is true, whatever is honorable, whatever is right, whatever is pure, whatever is lovely, whatever is of good report, if there is any excellence and if anything worthy of praise, dwell on these things (Philippians 4:8).*

Practice *staying there* until God tells you it is time to come out.

PRAYER: *Father, as I stand under the waterfall of your anointing, I ask that you would massage my heart with the oil of your Holy Spirit. I thank you for your anointing. Instruct me so that I may use wisely the gifts you have given me. I pray in Jesus' name. Amen.*

THE WILDERNESS

THE WILDERNESS

You've stood under the waterfall. You've been saturated and filled with the Holy Spirit. Out of the blue you find yourself standing on a plateau. Ahead you see nothing but desert. You turn around to look for the valley and it seems to be moving farther and farther out of sight. Suddenly you panic as you realize you are in a wilderness.

Aloud you ask yourself, "What am I doing here? How did I get here?"

If you have experienced an anointing shower, get ready. The Holy Spirit may lead you immediately into the wilderness. After Jesus was baptized he was straight away led into the wilderness.

Then Jesus, being filled with the Holy Spirit, returned from the Jordan and was led by the Spirit into the wilderness (Luke 4:1).

This was the time He was anointed to begin His miraculous ministry. But first He was led into the wilderness and there He was tempted by the devil. If you know the story you know he did not succumb to the temptations.

A wilderness is made up of different regions. Symbolically it represents many things. It has very dry places. It includes rocky plateaus and desolate mountain areas. There is no abundance of greenery or growth in a wilderness. You may run across an occasional oasis, but you will still be in a desert-like place. A wilderness is one of those places where you will not want to stay. Yet to accomplish *His* purpose, God may lead you into one.

Your wilderness may encompass your home, your job, or your association with unsaved family members. It may even include your church.

How many Christians are unhappy in their church? You want to leave and go somewhere else, but you don't know where to go. Unfortunately, God may not want you to leave where you are. He might need you to *stay there* in the wilderness church.

When the preached word is diluted and compromised, when the pulpit becomes a place for the pastor's personal agenda, or when a church is divided because a matter has not been dealt with according to scripture, a church can become a wilderness. For a believer who loves God, there are a multiplicity of harms that can make a church a wilderness place.

Why would God want you to stay in such a place? Could it be you have been chosen by Him to guide others out? Perhaps like John the Baptist, you are in there crying for repentance. Perhaps you are an oasis in the wilderness. By that, I mean seeing you will brighten someone's day. They look for you to share a word of encouragement, or give a hug. Perhaps it is the place God has chosen to prepare you for an even greater task. Since God's thoughts are higher than our own, there could be hundreds of reasons why He might have you in a wilderness church.

· But until *He* tells you to leave the church you are attending, *stay there*. God would not want you without a church home nor would He have you running from church to church. What good is your gift to the body if you are not stable?

When it is time for you to leave where you are He will direct you. Remember God has a way of confirming His word. Wait for confirmation.

Maybe you are the only one in your family who is saved. Because of the ungodly lifestyle of your relatives you would rather not attend family functions. That is a wilderness situation for you, a rocky terrain, and you'd like to pick up one of the rocks and hurl it at Uncle Johnny or Cousin Bert, or even Mom, or Dad. No one there respects your standing as a Christian. It would be easy enough not to be around those people. After all, you already have a circle of Christian friends who have quite a few believers in their family.

Do you realize that a wilderness is also a remote area? It is sometimes illustrated as an isolated region. It may consist of miles and miles of desert land. You might have to travel quite a ways to get through it. It can take years to complete the journey. You may be the only Christian in your family right now, but you were not always a Christian. Someone led you out of your wilderness of sin. Whether your family realizes it or not, you are their guide out of the wilderness. Attend those family reunions, barbecues, birthday parties, and showers. If you are not on hand when Uncle Johnny or Aunt Mary is ready to journey out how will they find their way?

19

"It's Monday morning and here I am again, among these heathens. God can't you find me a job where there are other Christians? I've witnessed to these people until I am blue in the face. They are never going to get saved."

If you have ever felt like that then my question to you is—have you ever heard about a man named Jesus?

This man did not say, "Father, I am not going to die for them because they are not worth it."

He did not say, "They will never accept me."

Instead he said, "Father, forgive them for they do not know what they are doing."

Today that statement might be articulated as, "They just don't get it!"

The people of Jesus' day did not understand the full ramifications of their acts when they crucified Him.

But we speak God's wisdom in a mystery, [even] the wisdom that hath been hidden, which God foreordained before the worlds unto our glory: which none of the rulers of this world hath known: for had they known it, they would not have crucified the Lord of glory (1 Corinthians 2:7-8).

As Solomon said, "There is nothing new under the sun."

Sinners today still don't understand or consider the full consequences of their sins.

Although a place of employment among the heathens may seem to be a wilderness, it is also a mission field. If you are the only Christian on your job, you have been ordained a missionary. Tell all your friends about your newfound "calling." Exhibiting a Christ-like behavior in your work place can be more effective than words. Actions usually speak volumes above words.

Far too many Christians are married to unbelievers. It isn't important at this stage whether you are a Christian and you married an unbeliever, or neither of you was saved and one converted to Christianity after the marriage. You find that your wilderness is right there in your home. You may want to leave but God is telling you to *stay there.* I am not talking about staying in a marriage where you or your children are being abused. Physical and psychological abuse both has long-term effects. Seek shelter if necessary to escape an abusive situation. What I am addressing is a spiritual matter, a disjointing of soul and spirit between a husband and a wife.

If you look around you will see a larger number of women in churches than you do men. I realize there are couples where the husband is a Christian and the wife is not. Please understand, because I have a burden for women, the next few words will be addressed to them.

If you are in an unloving, lonely marriage what I am about to say will be a hard pill to swallow. Consider however, these are not my words but they come from God's word.

But to the married I give instructions, not I, but the Lord. A wife should not leave her husband. But if she does leave, she must remain

21

unmarried, or else be reconciled to her husband. The husband should not divorce his wife.

But to the rest I say, not I but the Lord, that if any brother has a wife who is an unbeliever, and she consents to live with him, he must not divorce her. And the woman who has an unbelieving husband, who consents to live with her, she must not send her husband away. For the unbelieving husband is sanctified through his wife, and the unbelieving wife is sanctified through her believing husband; for otherwise your children are unclean, but now they are holy (1 Corinthians 7:10-14).

The short and the long of it is God telling you to *stay there.* You may recognize the fact that you are in a wilderness because of your circumstances (that of being unevenly yoked). However your unbelieving mate does not understand that he, or she, is in a wilderness called "sin."

It is especially important to be faithful in prayer when you are in this type of situation. God gave marriage as a gift. He could have created the woman the same way he created a man. He did it His way because He wanted to emphasize unity, harmony, and agreement. They all mean the same thing. Just as Israel was to be an example of a godly people to the surrounding nations, Christian couples should exemplify God's principle in marriage. Prayer and fasting will empower you during your journey as you stand in the gap for your mate.

The periodic discovery of an oasis will help you to survive in the wilderness. An oasis is a fertile place, a place of growth. Even in a wilderness there is a venue of beauty, a place of rejuvenation. Your oasis may be your time away from home attending a Christian conference. Boy, the mountain top experience you had there made you want to stay. But unless you've reached the end of your journey you will have to continue on through the wilderness. Don't be discouraged. The Israelites eventually came out (not all, but the faithful) and you will too.

Vegetation needs water to thrive in a wilderness. You will need water to thrive in your wilderness. God's word is water to a thirsty Christian.

Blessed are they, which do hunger, and thirst after righteousness: for they shall be filled (Matthew 5:6).

God will meet your need in the wilderness, if you stay focused on Him.

THE OUTCOME OF CHOICE

Without realizing it, there are times when we go into the wilderness voluntarily—not intentionally, but still it is of our own accord. We do this when we make bad choices.

A desert is a very dry place. I remember once when I was in the wilderness. I guess you can say I went there voluntarily. Instead of taking time for daily prayer, I prayed sporadically, giving in to the busyness of my day. I didn't set aside time for my Bible reading. What should have been my quiet time was filled with television time.

Before I knew it I had wandered into this dry place and mountains of desolation surrounded me.

A mountain called "attitude" loomed up before me. There were mountains of "indecision" and "stupidity." No matter what direction I turned, there stood a mountain. Not being conscious of when I arrived in the wilderness, finding my way out was a struggle.

After praying, I'd get up off my knees still feeling empty. I couldn't seem to hear from the Lord. I made poor business decisions during this time. My appetites were out of control. I knew the Bible contained the map that showed the way out; so everyday I searched it for direction.

One day it led me to an oasis. A man was sitting among the flora. He beckoned me. I sat down. An hour later I stood up. With tears in my eyes I thanked the Lord for communing with me and showing me the way out of the wilderness. Like the Samarian woman, I wanted to run and tell everyone "Come, come see a man." But I knew that I could not bring anyone into the intimacy which I had just experienced with the Lord. It would be up to them to encounter the Lord for themselves.

God was waiting. I had only to ask with a repentant heart and a sincere desire for *His* presence. I learned a valuable lesson. You cannot live your life any old way and expect God to be at your beck and call when you have time for Him, even if you are a Christian.

James says, *Count it all joy when you fall into various trials, knowing that the testing of your faith produces patience. But let patience have its perfect work, that you may be perfect and complete, lacking nothing. If any of you lacks wisdom, let him ask of God, who gives to all liberally and without reproach, and it will be given to him. But let him ask in faith, with no doubting, for he who doubts is like a wave of the sea driven and tossed by the wind. For let not that man suppose that he will receive anything from the Lord. But he is a double-minded man, unstable in all his ways (James 1:2-8).*

Dip into the oasis of God's word.

Often Jesus would go off by Himself to pray. Sometimes He would go to the wilderness.

So He Himself often withdrew into the wilderness and prayed (Luke 5:16).

Prayer is an oasis in the wilderness. *Stay there* until you hear a word from the Lord. He will guide you through and eventually guide you out. If you are in there to guide someone else out, the Lord will hold your hand as you hold on to theirs. Stop looking at your wilderness as a bad place and think purpose, God's purpose—for you.

I want to warn you, be certain it is God leading you out. You might be so desperate to run away from your home, or leave your job, or resign from your church that you *think* you hear God telling you it's okay. Run. Run as fast as you can.

25

I know a woman who hears only what she wants to hear from God. He tells her she is right and everyone else is wrong. And if she wants to leave one church and join another, God always says it's okay.

Coincidently, He directs her to the church she has already decided to join. In case you didn't catch the irony, be certain you are fulfilling the Lord's desires for your life and not your own.

The journey through a wilderness will become very disheartening at times. You may think you see a way to relieve your problem, but it is the wrong way. Suicide is never God's way out.

Nothing can mature a Christian like a wilderness experience. It can be a break-you or make-you situation. But don't allow the experience to break you—don't you dare. Trust God. Just as you think you're not going to make it, an oasis will come into your view. *Stay there*, meditate, pray, cry if necessary, but wait on the Lord to direct you.

When you come through your time of testing, whether it was for your sake or the sake of another, the reward will be awesome, because our God is an AWESOME GOD.

PRAYER: *Dear God, please forgive me for the times I failed to trust you. I allowed anxiety to control my life. Because I took my eyes off of you, my problems overwhelmed me. My method of fixing things seemed to make matters worse. In my heart I am struggling with feelings that I know are not pleasing to you. Jesus, I know you understand feelings of despair. I also know that if I am honest with you, you will help me. I realize now that I was never alone in the wilderness. You were there all the time. Thank you for being the God of another chance. In Jesus' name I pray. Amen.*

THE RAINBOW

Envision a huge coliseum. Hanging from the ceiling of this magnificent structure are dozens of scarves. There is an open skylight in the ceiling. A gentle wind is causing the scarves to sway back and forth as if they are dancing on the wings of the wind.

The scarves are made of silk, nylon, and taffeta. They embody every conceivable color. There's brilliant white, bright orange, royal blue, majestic purple, golden yellow, lavish pink, rosy red, dazzling silver, glittering gold, and greens of every hue. Some of the scarves are a myriad of colors.

The doors of the coliseum fling open. Enter men and women of every nationality. They each leap up and pluck a scarf from the air. The music begins to play. It's a beautiful praise song by a well-known artist. In concert, they begin to worship the Lord in the dance. Waving their scarves in the air, the dancers swirl around and around. Periodically a few of them will pause and bow down in admiration. As they dance, Jehovah Raah, the God who sees all, watches. From heaven He observes a magnificent rainbow of colors. He hears the words of adoration and takes pleasure as He delights in their praise.

Have you ever praised the Lord in dance?

Being human there are times when you feel burdened, stressed and put upon. That is the time to rise up from your seat, put on some praise music, grab a scarf and dance.

There is a time to weep, and a time to laugh; a time to mourn, and a time to dance (Ecclesiastes 3:4).

In this chapter, I will be coming from a different standpoint in respect to *staying there.*

When you feel heavy it's time to get up and dance. When your life resembles a raging storm, it's time to dance. The bright colors of your scarf will produce an exuberant effect in your spirit. Listen to the words of the music you chose. Allow the words to minister to you as you focus on the Lord and His goodness. Worship Him as you glide and bow and leap. Worship Him as your arms sway back and forth. Worship Him as you gently move from side to side. Worship Him in the dance.

Compare your scarf to a rainbow. A rainbow is the reflection of sunlight created by a curtain of falling rain, which produces an intermixture of colors in the form of an arc. A rainbow is the sign that a storm has passed. It is a reminder of a covenant God made with Noah concerning the earth and all living things.

Thus I establish my covenant with you: Never again shall all flesh be cut off by the waters of the flood; never again shall there be a flood to destroy the earth And God said: This is the sign of the covenant which I make between Me and you, and every living creature that is with you, for perpetual generations. I set my rainbow in the cloud, and it shall be for the sign of the covenant between Me and the earth. It shall be, when I bring a cloud over the earth, that the rainbow shall be seen in the cloud (Genesis 9:11-14).

Believers in Christ Jesus are in a covenant relationship with God. When you see a rainbow it should remind you of the covenant.

THE SON MAKES THE DIFFERENCE

As I write I begin to think of what a cloudy day means to me. On a cloudy day I get the blahs. A cloud of gloom and doom seem to accompany me wherever I go. If I am going through any sort of turmoil, on a cloudy day it is magnified. However, I love the sunshine. I feel good on a sunny day. I'm more energetic and I seem to get more accomplished.

I think it is wonderful that the sovereign God set the rainbow in a cloud. This should serve to remind us that even when things don't look so bright, God has placed a rainbow in our midst. He has imparted peace and faith to His children. He has given us a pledge of eternal hope.

The rainbow is only visible when the sun is behind it. The SON of God is always behind us when we are in His will. God's will gives emphasis to obedience. His will is found in His word. We cannot live outside the will of God and expect Jesus to co-sign our way of life. Anyone who thinks so is in grave error.

Then your light will break out like the dawn, and your recovery will speedily spring forth; and your righteousness will go before you; the glory of the LORD will be your "rear" guard. Then you will call, and the LORD will answer; you will cry, and He will say, Here I am (Isaiah 58:8,9).

Take special note on this part of the verse...*and your righteousness will go before you; the glory of the LORD will be your "rear" guard. Then* [and only then] *you will call and the LORD will answer; you will cry, and He will say, here I am.*

The Prophet Isaiah is speaking to the Nation of Israel in this passage.

Whenever we call on God, He will also say to us, "Here I am." God is there even on your cloudy day. The appearance of a rainbow is likened to the glory of God.

Like the appearance of a rainbow in a cloud on a rainy day, so was the appearance of the brightness all around it. This was the appearance of the likeness of the glory of the LORD (Ezekiel 1:28).

Hang a scarf of many colors in your home to keep you in remembrance of God's rainbow and His covenant. If you don't own a large scarf, purchase one. If you can afford it, buy a colorful banner. It will not only serve to keep you in remembrance of the rainbow, but as you brandish it in praise, it will serve as a weapon of warfare.

WHY WARFARE?

For though we walk in the flesh, we do not war according to the flesh. For the weapons of our warfare are not carnal but mighty in God for pulling down strongholds, casting down arguments and every high thing that exalts itself against the knowledge of God, bringing every thought into captivity to the obedience of Christ (2 Corinthians 10:3-5).

Praise and worship infuriate Satan when he is not the one being worshipped. Waving a praise banner in the face of Satan would probably be much like waving a red cape in front of a bull. Personally, I believe Satan's fury would be a million times that of the bull.

Satan, known as Lucifer before the fall, was music. He was not mere music; he was the ultimate of praise in music.

You were in Eden, the garden of God. Every precious stone was your covering, the sardis, topaz, and diamond the beryl, onyx, and jasper, the sapphire, turquoise, and emerald with gold. The workmanship of your timbrels and pipes was prepared for you on the day you were created. You were the anointed cherub who covers; I established you; you were on the holy mountain of God; you walked back and forth in the midst of fiery stones. You were perfect in your ways from the day you were created, till iniquity was found in you. By the abundance of your trading you became filled with violence

35

within, and you sinned; therefore I cast you as a profane thing out of the mountain of God (Ezekiel 28:13-16).

Lucifer lost his rank, his post, and his mind. *How you are fallen from heaven, O Lucifer, son of the morning! How you are cut down to the ground, you who weakened the nations!*

For you have said in your heart I will ascend into heaven, I will exalt my throne above the stars of God I will also sit on the mount of the congregation.

On the farthest sides of the north I will ascend above the heights of the clouds, I will be like the Most High (Isaiah 14:12-14).

Anyone who exalts himself, or herself above God, is truly to be judged insane. Satan hates the fact that you have been placed in his stead. You hold a coveted position. You have been given the honor of being a worshipper of the Most High. It is your privilege to praise Him. Allow me to draw a parallel of Satan's attitude toward you.

How would you feel if you were fired from your job and a co-worker was placed in your position? Although the person who replaced you was in no way responsible for your getting fired, you would probably feel some hostility toward them. You would love to see them fail in order to show your ex-boss what a mistake he or she made by dismissing you.

Satan would love to shake his fist in the face of Jesus and say, "See how foolish you were to die for them."

Ephesians 4:26 entreats us to *give no place to the devil.* A spirit of praise will neutralize Satan.

36

To emphasize what I said earlier, there is no (earthly) fury to compare to Satan's. He knows he is a defeated foe. However, he does not want you to know it. You will suffer if you allow him to keep you in a state of depression and abandonment,. He will cause you to experience defeat, along with himself. This can ultimately lead to your downfall.

The thief does not come except to steal, and to kill, and to destroy. I have come that they may have life, and that they may have it more abundantly (John 10:10).

Don't take the phrase...*that they may have it more abundantly,* lightly. The word abundant applies to living beyond measure, above the ordinary. Christian living is not to be measured on an ordinary scale, but on an extraordinary one, because of the power of the indwelling Holy Spirit. That is what the Lord wants for His children, and from His children.

The rainbow contains more colors than are visible to our eyes. But we don't see them because of the way they blend into one another. God created man and He fashioned us in many different colors.

We come in black, white, red, yellow, and different shades of brown. When God sees those He created dancing and waving their scarves in praise, He sees a rainbow of covenant people worshipping Him.

Dance. Don't stay there in a fixated state of depression. God has the power to make the darkness light. And He will do it for you.

And I will bring the blind by a way that they knew not; I will lead them in paths that they have not known: I will make darkness light before them, and crooked things straight. These things will I do unto them, and not forsake them (Isaiah 42:16).

Depression is darkness. Halleluiah anyhow, victory is yours. Be glad. Brandish your scarf in the face of the enemy and dance, dance, dance. If for some reason you are unable to physically dance, be assured that nothing can stop your spirit from leaping when you remember the promises of God. For it is in your spirit where true worship begins. Before you lift your hands to the Lord, you must first lift your heart. Just like sin begins with a thought, so does worship.

Through praise, through worship, through the dance, through desire, determine to have a rainbow day, a day of beauty and abundance.

PRAYER: *My Father, I thank you for the beauty of the rainbow. It reminds me that your promises are forever. In your word you say your covenant you will not break nor will you alter that which comes from your lips. Teach me to praise and worship you in my heart, with my body, and in my spirit, so that I will be wholly yours. Help me to be true in all the things I have promised you. These things I ask in Jesus' name. Amen.*

THE PATH

You will show me the path of life. In Your presence is fullness of joy. At Your right hand are pleasures forevermore (Psalm 16: 1).

The Path, may it be paramount in your mind and in your spirit.

In the story of *The Waterfall,* I alluded to those who may have had difficulty seeing themselves in the valley or imagining themselves under the waterfall. Could it be they found experiencing the presence of God to be unfamiliar territory?

I pray *The Path* will lead you to a place of intimacy. Though once you've moved up to that level in your relationship with God, it will be difficult for you to interrupt your time with Him in order to go about your daily tasks. But since the word of God tells us to do all things decently and in order, the daily tasks must be done.

Hopefully the imaginary journey you are about to embark upon will aid you in your pursuit of intimacy. (Of course, I am assuming that you desire to have intimacy with God.)

We were created to have intimate fellowship with God. God wasn't lonely; He had a host of angels. But He knew the joy we would receive from communing with Him. Having an intimate relationship with the Lord will not shield you from heartbreak or injury. But the results—you will be the recipient of great blessings.

41

Intimacy develops the relationship between you and God. It facilitates you becoming satisfied with what He has given you. *His* desires for you will grow to be your desires.

The Psalmist puts it this way, *Delight yourself in the Lord and He will give you the desires of your heart.*

Commit your way to the Lord, trust also in Him, and He will do it. He will bring forth your righteousness as the light and your judgment as the noonday. Rest in the LORD and wait patiently for Him (Psalm 37:4,5).

In a word, delighting in God will transform you and bring about a change in your heart. The path on which you will travel to get there is not a difficult one to follow. All you need is a map.

A path is any beaten way. It is also defined as a course or a station in life. Have you ever taken a walk through the forest? You stroll along listening to the sounds of the birds, and the groundhogs flittering back and forth. Periodically you glance down to avoid tripping over a rock. The sun shining through the maze of trees offers just enough light to make the forest appear mystical. You come across a fallen tree and cautiously step over it. Continuing down the trail a mile or so, you come to a path which winds around a steep hill.

Immediately you know that is not the direction you want to take. The fear of falling causes you to turn and seek another direction. You spy two more paths. You pick the one to your left and follow it for about two hundred feet before you realize that it dead-ends at a ridge. Returning from the ridge you wish you had doubled back to where you saw the fallen tree. From there you could have found your way out of the forest. Instead you chose to try several different trails. You were sure that one of them would be a shortcut leading you out. None of them were.

Now you are so confused you can't remember which path will lead you back to the tree. Do you continue to seek a way out? Or do you sit down and cry hoping someone, anyone, will come along and help you?

When you take the wrong paths in life you come to dead ends. When you are so afraid of failure you don't try—dead end. You may be sure of your salvation, but you don't know what your gift is—dead end. You are very active in your church yet you don't find working there very rewarding—dead end. You realize you are in an unfulfilling relationship and you are at a loss as to what to do—dead end. What's lacking is intimacy with the Lord. You are operating by rote. You are enmeshed in "good works." Good works are fine as long as they do not take the place of "intimacy."

Stop crying, stand up, and look over to your right.

THE JOURNEY

Do you see the sign posted on the big tree? Notice the arrow pointing straight ahead. Move in a little closer. There, now you can read it. It says, THIS WAY TO INTIMACY. Yes, it was there all the

43

time. Don't feel bad because you didn't see it before now. I'm sure this is not the first time you missed a sign from God.

Go in the direction the arrow is pointing. It will carry you out of the forest and lead you to the main road; get on it. There are some paths that run off the main one. So I'll draw you a map. I hope you won't get lost. You will come across some detours. DO NOT TAKE THEM. The signs have been put there as a distraction. You must stay focused.

Look at your map. See the area I marked with an X? That is where you are now. Travel about five hundred feet until you come to a bend in the road. You will see a sign pointing to PRAYER PLACE. It will be a small clearing characterized by an arch of trees. *Stay there* awhile. Normally, this time of day a couple of fellows called Confession and Repentance happen along. You might want to make their acquaintance. But don't spend all your time with them. You will want to give equal time to a pair known as Thanksgiving and Adoration.

After you have spent some time in PRAYER PLACE, continue on. A mile or so down the path is a place called HUNGER HIGHWAY; it runs up through the NEW KING JAMES MOUNTAINS. I hear the geography is beautiful. Be sure to take notice as you travel through. Some people find the mountains difficult to get through, but I believe if you take your time you'll become a seasoned mountain climber.

44

Look at your map again. Do you see the red dot near the bottom? This is an area where you need to stay on guard concerning those distractions. The red dot shows you where EXPECTATION INN is found. They serve quite a feast at the Inn. The owner himself does the actual serving. They have a source of water there that is like no other. They tell me it will satisfy your thirst for righteousness. I'm also told peace and faith is sumptuously dished out. Though it seems wisdom is their most popular appetizer. And they never run out of it—amazing.

As you dine, think of the beautiful scenery you came across in the NEW KING JAMES MOUNTAINS.

<u>Peace</u> I leave with you, My <u>peace</u> I give to you; not as the world gives do I give to you. Let not your heart be troubled, neither let it be afraid (John 14:27).

He stores up sound <u>wisdom</u> for the upright; He is a shield to those who walk uprightly (Proverbs 2:7)

For we walk by <u>faith,</u> not by sight (2 Corinthians 5:7).

Feast. Nourish your spirit. Meditate.

As soon as you have dined sufficiently you need to get back on the road. Remember to keep your eyes on the pathway. Don't stray from the main road. Continue looking forward. Your obedience will be rewarded. If you've made it this far you're almost there.

Travel down two more miles and you will come to a place called QUIET TIME JUNCTION. This is where you need to spend a lot of time. This is the last place wherein your map directs you. If you stay here long enough you won't miss God when He arrives. He will direct you from here, you may not be sure in which direction to go. See that log over there? Have a seat and wait.

Abruptly the silence is broken and you hear someone speak. You look around, but there's no one there. You remain quiet. A thought comes to mind. You turn to your left and you see a signpost. You wonder why you hadn't noticed it when you first arrived. It was just another missed sign from God, it happens.

Now you get up and walk over to the signpost. The sign reads WELCOME YOU ARE IN THE PLACE OF INTIMACY, POPULATION TWO. You look down and see a Bible lying on the ground; you pick it up and walk back to the log. As you sit down another thought pops into your head. You open the Bible and begin to read.

As the Father loved Me, I also have loved you; abide in My love. If you keep My commandments, you will abide in My love, just as I have kept My Father's commandments and abide in His love. These things I have spoken to you, that My joy may remain in you, and that your joy may be full. This is My commandment, that you love one another as I have loved you (John 15:9-12).

Suddenly you realize the thoughts were not *your* thoughts at all, but it was God speaking. And in an intimate moment He said, "I love you." God will continue to tell you through His word that He loves you. And as you mature, you will hear Him say it in your spirit.

Now that you have found your way to INTIMACY, God will be expecting you to return. He's there day and night. Drop by anytime. And you know what? He is full of information and answers so there is no telling what He will have for you on your next visit. Let me remind you how to get there, God does not want you to get lost. Keep in mind, there are no shortcuts.

First, you go to PRAYER PLACE. From there you keep straight until you pick up HUNGER HIGHWAY. If you deviate from PRAYER you will not reach it. HUNGER will take you through NEW KING JAMES MOUNTAINS. When you come out of the mountains, instantly you will see EXPECTATION INN. Make a stop there. Your journey thus far should have given you quite an appetite. Look forward to being served by the owner Himself. When you leave, go two more miles down the road until you come to QUIET TIME JUNCTION. Once you have arrived you will be in the place of INTIMACY. Got it?

Oh, one thing I forgot to mention. The main road you were traveling on when you began your journey, was called FELLOWSHIP ROAD. Aren't you glad you didn't detour? Was it worth staying on the right path? It certainly was for me.

PRAYER: *Dear Lord, I have failed in answering your call so many times. Yet you continue to love me. You have waited patiently for me to come to that place of intimacy. Help me to love you with my whole heart, so that when I arise in the mornings, I will seek your face and the touch of your hand. I am so blessed that you would desire to have an intimate relationship with me. I pray that this will only be the beginning of many talks we will have. When we are alone teach me how to be still so that I may reap the benefits of our time together. Help me not to wander off from you again. I know now that you have been my constant companion. I ask your forgiveness as I attempt to do better. I pray with expectations. Thank you for desiring fellowship with me. Amen.*

THE STAR

~~~~~~

And God made the two great lights, the greater light to govern the day, and the lesser light to govern the night; He made the stars also. And God placed them in the expanse of the heavens to give light on the earth, and to govern the day and the night, and to separate the light from the darkness; and God saw that it was good (Genesis 1:16-18).

Since the fall of man, God has desired a people who would set an example of godly living. In the world, Christians are the designated people. We are to be the governing lights that lead unbelievers out of the darkness of sin. Instead, many Christians are themselves being influenced by worldly principles.

The Bible tells us that in the beginning God spoke to light and light appeared. The Bible further states that God made the stars and He set them in place. Can you picture God fervently placing each star exactly where He wanted it, distinguishing, and naming each one? He placed the North Star, and the Sirius, the Alpha Centauri, the Betelgeuse, and so on until all the stars were named and positioned.

He telleth the number of the stars; he called them all by their names. Great is our Lord, and of great power: his understanding is infinite (Psalm 147: 4,5).

51

Man may think he named the stars but somewhere along the line God told man their names (and man is still taking credit for what God has done).

Because He is God and He is omnipresent (everywhere at all times), creating the heavens probably took a matter of seconds.

Think about it, how long does it take to say, "Let there be?"

God called the place in which He set the stars, heaven. In creation God put everything exactly where He wanted it and everything God created stayed in its place, everything except man.

And the LORD God commanded the man, saying, Of every tree of the garden you may freely eat; but of the tree of the knowledge of good and evil you shall not eat, for in the day that you eat of it you shall surely die (Genesis 2:16,17).

So when the woman saw that the tree was good for food, that it was pleasant to the eyes, and a tree desirable to make one wise, she took of its fruit and ate. She also gave to her husband with her, and he ate (Genesis 3:6).

On earth, God placed a man called Adam in a heavenly environment known to us as the Garden of Eden. Adam and his wife sinned by disobeying God. They ate fruit from the tree of the knowledge of good and evil after God had commanded them not to. When this happened they fell from their first estate, the domain in which God intended for all mankind to dwell.

Because Adam and his wife sinned they were cast out of the Garden, never to return. God loved His creation too much to allow them to live forever in the destruction that He knew sin was going to bring. Therefore, He placed angels and a flaming sword in the midst of the garden to guard the tree of life. Adam and his woman forfeited the gift of immortality.

This is the account of how one man allowed sin to enter into a perfect world. And sin from that moment on has cast a dark shadow over the world. The brightest star could not shatter the darkness of sin. It would take a SON. But the omniscient God was already prepared to send Jesus. Through His son He would once again bring order, and give mankind hope. Man would have a choice. He could choose to live in the darkness sin breeds or he could be a light in the darkness.

The Holy Spirit was given by God to empower us and also to keep us from being snared by sin and succumbing to the darkness. But He can only keep us from sin if we are yielded to Him.

Because of sin or the circumstances of life, we find ourselves in situations that are hard to deal with and we search for an escape. Escape is the ability to free one's self from captivity. However, how do you free yourself? When you are held captive it takes someone who is already free to help you. Jesus came to free us from captivity.

Regrettably, even we as Christians allow ourselves to become ensnared. When we do, we often employ the wrong methodology trying to get free. Alcohol, drugs, and sex are commonly used escape mechanisms. One of the most deceptive means of escaping a problem is the use of sleep. Sleeping may seem innocent enough but if you develop an abnormal sleeping pattern it could be a doorway leading to depression. Depression will not only inhibit your private life it will also impede your effectiveness in ministry. Just as God designed the stars with a purpose in mind, you were designed for a much greater purpose. It is important that you don't let sin disrupt God's purpose for you.

Many times I have heard the declaration, "God's will" will be done. That is a very true statement if you are referring to His *sovereign will*. But God has a *moral will* for each one of us, and He will not violate our right to choose in order to accomplish His will for our lives.

Since God wants us to mirror the life of Jesus, there are three facts concerning stars that I would like to compare to the life of a Christian.

A SHINING EXAMPLE

Fact one, stars shine day and night but they can only be seen when the sky is dark.

The word of God tells us we are overcomers; therefore, God knew there would be situations in life we would have to overcome. Nothing comes upon one of God's children without His *permissive will*. When God allows trouble to come into our lives, He is giving us a perfect opportunity to shine. There will be periods of grief and despair. However, those times should not alter our very nature. Others should still see something different in the way we handle the quandaries of life.

And they that are wise shall shine as the brightness of the firmament; and they that turn many to righteousness as the stars forever and ever (Daniel 12:3,4).

The second fact is a star's energy source lies deep within it. Within the Christian lives a supreme source of power called the Holy Spirit.

No temptation has overtaken you except such as is common to man; but God is faithful, who will not allow you to be tempted beyond what you are able, but with the temptation will also make the way of escape, that you may be able to bear it (1 Corinthians 10:13).

The Holy Spirit is the one who enables us to endure trials. In the story of *The Wilderness,* I wrote about a place of employment being a wilderness experience. Maintaining a positive attitude in the workplace is a common trial for a lot of Christians. You prayed for a certain job and finally you got it. There is no doubt in your mind that God opened the door. After working for a few weeks you discover that you don't like your boss or the atmosphere in the work place. What is your solution to the problem? Do you quit (if you are able) and seek another source of income? Or do you remain, feeling trapped?

Have you considered why God placed you there? Have you forgotten; the Holy Spirit is your staying power.

Jesus had a choice when the soldiers came to the garden to arrest Him. He could have escaped the same as He did when the Jews wanted to kill Him.

Then took they up stones to cast at him: but Jesus hid himself, and went out of the temple, going through the midst of them, and so passed by (John 8:59).

Jesus could have escaped His crucifixion. Instead He prayed, *Father, if it is Your will, take this cup away from Me; nevertheless not My will, but Yours, be done (Luke 22:42).*

And when they placed Jesus on the cross, although He had all the power He needed to come down from it, He stayed.

Adam was in a beautiful garden, a place of perfection. Which of us would not want to remain in a place of beauty, a trouble-free place where everything we need would be at our fingertips? If Adam had known the consequence of his action maybe he would not have yielded to Satan so easily. Adam took no thought of having to leave the garden. He probably didn't think about it one way or the other. He gave in to the moment. Giving in to wrongdoing will often produce long-term consequences.

Jesus did not give in to the moment. He considered the future, our future. When you allow the Holy Spirit to work in you, you will be considerate of the future as well as the moment. Your continued presence in the workplace might bring about a change in the atmosphere. Yield to the source of power which lies deep within you. He will never lead you astray.

In comparison, the last fact is there's a slow change in a star once it begins to shine. The closer you are to your heavenly Father, the more you will radiate. Your focus will change. Your heart will change. There will be a change in your speech and your attitude about life.

In the beginning, I said the stars were stars only because God called them stars. The word of God identifies who we are also. We are called ambassadors (1Corinthians 5:20), we have been made heirs of Christ (Romans 8:17), as Christians we are of a royal family (1 Peter 2:9). Oftentimes, people associate their identity with their job or job title. Many identify with their position or their caste. Some see themselves only in the roles they assume. In the kingdom of God, you are more than a role, or a position, or a title. You are a bright and shining star.

If you have been placed in a governing position of authority, such as an executive in the workplace, or a pastor over a flock, remember it was God who allowed you to be there. Don't become power hungry, but practice humility. I've heard humility defined as "power under control." For me that says it all.

If you are a stay at home housewife don't feel inferior to the businesswomen who go into the office everyday. Avail yourself to them; offer to baby-sit. Thank God for giving you the opportunity to be a nurturer for their children as well as your own. Exactly like the stars, God designated a place for each one of us so His purpose in and through us would be fulfilled.

The next time you look up and see a star, consider, are you a radiant presence in a darkened world? Do you depend on the Holy Spirit to fuel your spirit? Are you where God wants you? Are you content and willing to *stay there* until He repositions you?

Let your light so shine before men, that they may see your good works, and glorify your Father which is in heaven (Matthew 5:16).

Real Christians are the real superstars. Shine on.

PRAYER: *Lord, I ask that you would make me a blessing in someone's life today. I pray that the brightness of my countenance will lift someone's spirit. Even though I am going through something myself, I ask that you give me an opportunity to share your word with someone. Lord, speak to me as I minister so I will rightly divide your word. Help me to help them see that they have a purpose in your scheme of things. All this I ask in Jesus' name. Amen.*

THE BRIDGE

In the distance I see a gray wooden bridge. It is a short bridge, only a few feet long. It's the type of bridge you find in rural areas. It's made of slats and shaped in an arch. There is a wooden rail on each side of the bridge. A shallow brook flows beneath it and rows of flowers grow along its sides. On the bridge, a young couple stands close together. They give the impression of being very much in love. Maybe they are newlyweds. As they stand side-by-side facing westward, the sun begins to set. They're not engaged in conversation; they're merely standing in the middle of the bridge, silently gazing toward the west. He has his arm around her shoulder. Clearly they are very much in love.

"God," I asked, "what is the significance of the couple on the bridge? What is the focal point? Is it the couple or the bridge itself?

Unlike the waterfall, the rainbow, or the stars, the bridge is not of nature. Neither is it a created thing, it is a man-made object. It's synthetic. What does any of this have to do with *staying there*?"

The couple has not moved. The sun is beginning to set and still they stand, quietly facing the west. From the expression on their faces they appear to be of one mind in a faraway place.

61

The sky turns orange as the sun sets. Still, they stand as if some magical spell will be broken if they move even the slightest. They watch as the sky goes from sunset to twilight. As it darkens to dusk they turn toward one another and smile. While I stand in the distance watching, they kiss. Without speaking a word, hand in hand they stroll off the bridge. I watch them until they were out of sight. I look back toward the bridge and wonder. Was the bridge symbolic of an earlier period in their life? For a moment were they able to relive it? Nevertheless they were at peace as they left. The smile between them appeared to be their way of silently telling one another, it was time to go.

I think I am beginning to understand. The couple had come to the bridge to reflect on a time gone by. Being there helped them to recall some magical moment in their past. Yet they seemed content with the present.

A NIGHT TO REMEMBER

Has God ever done something in your life that was so extraordinary, you wanted to relive it again and again? It may have been something so incredible you were almost afraid to share it, for fear people would think you were crazy or fabricating. I will tell you about one of my incredible times.

Believe it or not—I've seen the shape of snowflakes.

There was a time in my life when I detested winter. I would grumble whenever it arrived. The occurrence I am about to reveal changed my outlook forever.

One wintry night as the fresh snow was falling, I walked through my house turning out the lights. I started in the front and proceeded to move toward the rear. Most people probably would have started in the rear and worked forward, but for some reason I began to turn off the lights as I went, knowing I would have to walk back through a completely dark house. There was a full moon that night so I supposed I would be able to see my way back without the aid of artificial lighting.

Located at the rear of the house is our breakfast room. Seeing there was no light on in the breakfast room, the last light to be turned out was in the kitchen. As I turned out the light in the kitchen, I looked toward the breakfast room. In there we have a large sliding glass window. Suddenly the snow falling against the moonlit backdrop caught my eye. I moved toward the window and stood there. As I stood, God began to speak to me. I don't remember what I heard, but I remember the snowflakes.

Their appearance was large enough for me to see the different shapes. I stood there in the dark watching them slowly fall, as if allowing me to see each one individually. I don't know how long I stood there; I believe it was quite a while. I did not want the marvelous sight to cease. It was a magnificent picture representing the splendor of God's handiwork. It occurred to me, how could anyone hate wintertime when it afforded such beauty.

Has God ever spoken to you through nature? If He has then you understand.

The next morning I put on some warm clothing and went outside. I stood in my front yard looking up and marveling at how the white snow sat so perfectly on the bare tree limbs. I watched as rays of sunshine sparkled and danced on top of its softness. After that night I never again said, "I hate winter." God had shown me the different shape of snowflakes.

For a period of time after that, when it snowed I would stand in my breakfast room, in the dark, trying to recreate that night. But it never took place again.

My account of the snowflake may not sound very "spiritual" to some, but it conveys the fact that God is interested in our attitudes and our thoughts about everything. He wanted me to appreciate that which I had professed to hate—winter. After all, He assigned the seasons. Many times we forget that the smallest things matter to God. We fail to remember that the carelessness of our words is of concern Him.

The things God has shown me are not occurrences that happen daily, but they have happened. There have been other phenomena in my life having to do with my Heavenly Father. I know some may have a hard time dealing with this, so I am going to share one more incident where there were witnesses, twelve witnesses to be exact.

THE RETREAT

Our ladies Bible study had put together a retreat. Twelve ladies had signed up to go. For a few of them it was their first time on a retreat. Before I continue I must say again, *OUR GOD IS AN AWESOME GOD.* I still get excited thinking about what God did on that retreat.

There were quite a few of us who had experienced amazing things from the Lord. But there was one woman in particular who had not. As I said, this was the first retreat ever for a few of the ladies.

A woman, I'll call her Anna, and her daughter was among the newcomers. To begin I must go back prior to our leaving. I believe strongly in prayer. I believe the only way to make something successful is to ask God for guidance. I believe in being obedient when He directs me (although I know I sometimes fail in that area).

I had prayed for every little thing concerning this retreat, including who were to be roommates. After I knew who was to be in the room with whom, I called each one to tell them who their roomy would be. I called Anna and informed her that her roommate would be Betty (I'll call her Betty, I don't want to use real names). She was very quiet for a moment.

The next words out of her mouth were, "I thought my daughter and I would be in a room together."

Now I was momentarily silent. I stammered slightly as I told her I had prayed about it and Betty was to be her roommate.

If we are truthful, there are times in our lives when, even though we know the Lord has directed us to do something a certain way, we still falter. Immediately upon hanging up I was tempted to call Anna back and tell her she and her daughter could be roommates. In fact I did call her back.

Fortunately when I explained why I was calling, she said, "It's alright, I trust your judgment, I'll room with Betty."

I felt a little ashamed. God had given me the room assignments and I was going to change them to appease someone. I was glad that Anna didn't allow me to do that, especially after what happened at the retreat.

The retreat began on Thursday evening and was to end after our Sunday morning worship service. On this particular retreat, it was decided that we would fast from meat and desserts. Our diet was to consist strictly of vegetables and fruit. At the beginning, there was a little grumbling about it, but it wasn't long before the ladies realized they felt better and had more energy. Getting up at five o'clock in the morning for prayer and praise was not as difficult.

Thursday went well. Everyone arrived safely. Each one unpacked and went to the dining room for supper. The place where we held the retreat prepared all of our meals; much to our surprise they were quite tasty. The variety of vegetables they offered was very appetizing.

After supper we met in our assigned area. We received our instructions and then departed to our rooms. There were thirteen of us, including our presenter. The ladies were two to a room and our workshop presenter had a room to herself.

On Friday, according to schedule, we arose and met in time for six o'clock prayer and praise. Afterwards we went to the dining room for breakfast, and from there we assembled for class. At the close of our morning session we had an hour break before we met for lunch. My roomy had gone for a walk on the beach and I retired to our room for some quietude. As I was preparing to pray, someone knocked on my door. It was Betty. She had come to tell what had transpired between her and Anna. Since I was their Bible study teacher and also instrumental in spearheading the retreat, I was the one they sought when there was a problem.

Betty told me that Anna had gone to her daughter's room and instructed her to pack because they were leaving. When Betty walked into the room and saw Anna packing, she asked her where she was going. Anna said she called home and her mother, who was taking care of Anna's grandson, told her the boy was sick. It was nothing more serious than a bad cold, but Anna was packing to leave.

Betty asked her, "Is that your daughter's grandmother you are talking about?"

She replied, "Yes."

Betty asked, "Is that your mother you are talking about?"

Anna replied, "Yes."

Betty said, "Anna, think about it, your mother raised you, she has a granddaughter, do you mean to tell me she does not know what to do for a child with a cold?"

While Anna was pondering the question, Betty started unpacking her bag. Anna went to her daughter's room and told her they were not leaving.

After listening to Betty I realized if Anna and her daughter had shared the same room, they would have been gone before anyone knew the difference. But this is not the end of the story.

The rest of Friday was uneventful, but then came Saturday. Saturday morning started out according to schedule (with prayer, praise, and breakfast afterwards). We attended morning session and had our free time following that. When we met for our afternoon session we were instructed to spend three hours being quiet before the Lord. We were not to speak to anyone or socialize with one another. The communion we were to have was to be with God, and only Him.

Three hours later when we came together again, there was expectancy in the room as each one was anxious to share her testimony. And every lady had one. Everyone expect Anna. Even Anna's daughter had a testimony to share. To some God had revealed Himself in nature. Others received a word from Him. A few had felt His touch. But when it came to Anna, she had not experienced anything. It was obvious to all that Anna felt aloof from the Lord. She had not experienced any revelation concerning Him. She felt as if something was wrong with her.

We attempted to console Anna as we told her that, God does not speak merely because we want to hear from Him. There are times when we wonder if He is even listening. But all Anna knew was, everyone, including her own daughter, had some experience with God and she had none.

The session ended and we went our separate ways until it was time for dinner. At dinner Anna was still a little downcast. I thought she would be better after a good night's sleep. Was I ever wrong!

After dinner my roommate and I were in our room discussing the goodness of God and the events of the day. Someone knocked on our door. I opened it and there stood Betty, only this time Anna was with her. At once, I knew something was wrong. Looking closely at Anna, I saw the problem. Anna's right eye was swollen. It was almost twice its normal size. My first thought was, oh boy why Anna? As they walked into the room I thought about how Anna already felt deserted by God.

"God, couldn't you have allowed this to happen to one of the other women? This was her first retreat and now it would probably be her last. Every woman here had more faith in you than Anna."

All this was going through my mind as Betty and Anna walked over to the bed to sit down.

Silently I began to pray, only God could help me comfort her. She had come to me for answers and I had none. Only a question for God, "Why Anna?"

Anna was in too much pain to cry. She didn't understand. For all appearances the other women were enjoying the retreat. She seem to be the only one not getting anything out of it—save an infected eye.

I told her to pray and ask God to heal her eye. I could not explain to her why this happened. I only knew that God was a God of purpose and plan, not coincidence and circumstance. I told her God loved her and she must trust Him.

I quoted, *All things work together for good to those who love God, to those who are the called according to His purpose (Romans 8:28).*

All the time I felt as if I was talking to someone who was too disgusted to receive any of this. I understood if this was the way she felt. There are times when you try to help someone and you are at a loss for words. The only thing you can do is try to encourage them from the word of God. Even if you feel the words are falling on deaf ears, the words you speak will sooner or later return to them.

The three of us ministered to Anna a few minutes longer. Afterwards we prayed for her eye to be healed. Anna thanked us and she and Betty returned to their room.

It had already been established that Sunday, being the last day of the retreat, was the day we would break our fast. We could eat meat, sweets, and anything else we desired. Knowing this, the ladies were looking forward to Sunday morning breakfast.

A HEALING

Sunday morning we met as usual for prayer and praise. I felt a little guilty. There we were in praise while Anna sat quietly in her chair dabbing her eye with a tissue. By this time everyone knew about Anna's eye. A few of the ladies laid hands on her as they prayed. Suddenly, amidst the prayers we heard Anna say, "I can see."

Each one turned to look at Anna. Right there before our eyes we saw God heal her. Slowly her swollen eye began to shrink. Within seconds her eye had returned to its normal size and color. As the rest of the ladies gathered around Anna, she began to cry.

Her only words were, "God healed me. God healed my eye."

There was no doubt in her mind that it was God. She felt her eye being healed. Anna had experienced her personal encounter with the Lord. Now she was more secure in her relationship with Him.

The praise that went up in that room would have moved the largest mountain. No one was interested in breakfast. But because breakfast had been prepared for us, I had to urge the ladies to go to the dining room.

Concerning the resurrection of Jesus, Paul writes, *For I delivered to you first of all that which I also received: that Christ died for our sins according to the Scriptures, and that He was buried, and that He rose again the third day according to the Scriptures, and that He was seen by Cephas, then by the twelve. After that He was seen by over*

71

five hundred brethren at once, of whom the greater part remain to the present, but some have fallen asleep (1 Corinthians 15:3-6).

You may find my story about the snowflake hard to believe, but that is all right, I know it happened. If Cephas (Peter) had been the only one to see Jesus before He ascended they probably wouldn't have believed him either. But just like Jesus was seen of the twelve, twelve saw the miraculous healing of Anna's eye. The twelve women on retreat at an Ohio resort in 1999.

You may wonder why would God cause Anna pain, only to heal her? Surely there were a lot of other ways to reveal Himself to her. Well, because He is God, He knew how to relate to Anna. He knew what He had to do to be real to her.

When you have a relationship with Jesus you will be shown and told things that will be hard for others to believe. In times of prayer, the presence of God will be so humbling, the spiritual realm will seem more real to you then this present world. The peace you will feel will be so overwhelming that you will not want to open your eyes and face your surroundings. You will want to *stay there*.

The occurrences of the phenomenal in one's life should not be difficult to believe when you remember it is an absolute supreme God bringing it to pass. In my life there have been supernatural occurrences that I have wanted to experience again and again. You may have had the same desire. But God will give you a fresh encounter with Him, which you will also want to relive.

Like the couple on the bridge we can only travel back mentally. No matter how great the desire, what we recreate in our mind does not compare to the actual event.

The couple on the bridge seemed to be thinking about a time long gone. Remembering seemed to satisfy them. Until the Lord chooses to reveal more of Himself to us we must be content with the moment and the memories of past phenomena. Jesus gave us access into the Kingdom of Heaven. He is the bridge between heaven and earth. If you stay close to Him, God will unveil the extraordinary. He will show you great and mighty things.

Oh give thanks unto Jehovah, call upon his name; make known among the peoples his doings.

Sing unto him, sing praises unto him; talk ye of all his marvelous works. Glory ye in his holy name: let the heart of them rejoice that seek Jehovah.

Seek ye Jehovah and his strength; seek his face evermore. Remember his marvelous works that he hath done, His wonders, and the judgments of his mouth (Psalm 105:1-5).

Staying close is the key. I guarantee His closeness will produce the magnificent and work the miraculous in your life. Jesus is the only source by which man and God can be united. He is the bridge that will take you from the ordinary to the extraordinary.

PRAYER: *Lord Jesus, thank you for giving me access to your Father. Today I pray for an increase in faith. I ask that someone will experience something miraculous in their life so all doubt of your miracle working power will be dispelled. If that someone is to be me, then I await your presence. I believe your word where it says that there is nothing too hard for you. Yet I find myself wavering when it comes to the difficulties of life. Please, Father, help my unbelief. Amen.*

THE BATTLEGROUND

THE BATTLEGROUND

I would like to introduce this part of my devotional by telling you why I called it the battleground instead of the battlefield. I began by typing The Battlefield, but the Lord kept saying *battleground.* I thought, what difference did it make? I will pass on that which was pointed out to me. There is a difference, fine line though it may be. All dry land is ground, but all dry land is not a field. A field is always ground, but ground may not necessarily be a field. Simple, huh?

The life of a Christian is an ongoing battle; therefore the term battleground seems more appropriate than battlefield. You can step out of a field, but you will still be on ground. There is no escaping the war, not if you are serious about your relationship with Christ. Oh, there will be times of R and R (rest and relaxation). There will be furloughs (recreation). But you will eventually have to return to the heat of the battle.

The Apostle Paul states it better than I when he writes, *We are troubled on every side, yet not distressed; we are perplexed, but not in despair; Persecuted, but not forsaken; cast down, but not destroyed (2 Corinthians 4:8,9).*

My questions to you: where do you find rest from a battle when the war is within you? How do you treat a wound that exceeds the realm of your physical reach? How do you forgive when you are unjustly accused?

Jeremiah asks, *Is there no balm in Gilead, and is there no physician there? Why then is there no recovery for the health of the daughter of my people? (Jeremiah 8:22)*

There was a balm in Gilead, so the question asked was rhetorical and meant to be thought provoking. The balm represented a symbol of spiritual healing. It was an extremely fragrant, resinous substance extracted from the balsam tree, which grew in Israel, and was used for the healing of the nations.

To rephrase the question, "Has Israel then no balm for *Herself?* Is there no physician in *Her* who can bind up *Her* wounds?"

Gilead was to be to Israel what Israel spiritually was to the nations.

So I ask again, "Where do you find rest from the battle when the war is within you? How do you treat a wound that exceeds the realm of your physical reach? How do you bring healing to others when you yourself stand in need of being healed? How do you achieve R and R?"

As Christians we have a Savior and a deliverer. We have a healer whose title is Jehovah Rapha. A well-known artist sang a song entitled *Wounded Soldier*. She opens up by singing, "See all the wounded."

In the song she speaks of ministering healing to the wounded and pouring the oil to bind their hurts.

In one of the refrains she sings, "Weakened from battle, Satan, crept in to take their lives."

James, the brother of Christ, asked, *Is anyone among you suffering? Let him pray. Is anyone cheerful? Let him sing psalms. Is anyone among you sick? Let him call for the elders of the church, and let them pray over him, anointing him with oil in the name of the Lord (James 5:13,14).*

Christians have an adversary whose name is Satan. He is the one who gains satisfaction when we hurt. He sees the weaknesses in our flesh and moves in for the kill. He sees the pain we are experiencing and magnifies it. You may wonder how can he do that when God is all-powerful? For God is the greatest power there is.

DART DAMAGE

Satan is a depraved strategist and one method he uses to accomplish his perverted goal is something I call "dart damage." I will try to give you a mental picture of Satan's tactics.

Customarily, each morning, Satan calls his hordes of demons together. Swiftly they gather, anxiously wanting to please their master. At their morning meeting he passes out pouches filled to the brim with darts. All the darts have a label. He hands out a list of names to each foul demon. After he gives them their assignment, they scurry off to carry out their mission. Eagerly anticipating his success, the evil demon approaches. Skillfully he readies his dart, he aims and he fires. He hits his target—you. The dart attacks your self-esteem. It carried a label that reads "unworthy." He fires again, planting the thought that God doesn't really love you. Surely, God would not have let the awful thing happen to you if He did. (*Surely* took place in Eden and is still being effectively used by Satan).

He'll fire a dart into a wound that is almost healed and suddenly you're afraid to trust again. There are thousands of these darts being fired and they all originate from a liar, a murder, and a thief.

When a person suffers a cruelty, an inability to recognize the real enemy causes them to lose their focus, misplace their loyalty, and live a defeated life. But let me remind you, there *is* a balm in Gilead. In other words there is healing for the broken hearted, the abused, the lonely, and the fearful.

But when the multitudes knew it, they followed Him; and He received them and spoke to them about the kingdom of God, and healed those who had need of healing (Luke 9:11).

He, in this Scripture, is Jesus, and *He* still has the power to heal those in need of healing. *He* is your R and R (restoration and refuge).

In congregations we sing songs of victory such as, *I Am On The Battlefield For My Lord* and *I Am A Soldier In The Army Of The Lord.* Many who sing these songs are, themselves, crippled or wounded. I don't mean physically, I mean emotionally and spiritually. The reality of this, reminds me of the old adage "physician heal thyself."

How can we fight the good fight of faith when we ourselves are wounded and in pain? It may be that the one who hurt you is dead and buried; nonetheless you are still suffering emotionally because of what they did to you years before.

Has there ever been a time when you were watching television and a spiritual application jumped out at you? I've had it happen to me several times.

When I was growing up there were not nearly as many cartoons about demons and spiritual entities as there are now. Of course, looking back, I must admit there was a bit of violence portrayed in the cartoons of the 1950's and 60's.

One of my favorite cartoons was *The Roadrunner*. The cartoon was set in the desert. The two main characters were the Roadrunner and a coyote named Wylie. The Roadrunner and Wylie Coyote were natural enemies. The coyote was perpetually after the Roadrunner. The Roadrunner would run from place to place making a "beep beep" sound, and the coyote would chase after him (the roadrunner can run up to fifteen miles per hour). I don't know what the coyote was going to do if he ever caught him because he never did. At least I never saw it.

Anyway, the Roadrunner was always getting the best of ole Wylie. Several times a day, Wylie Coyote would set an explosive trap for his nemesis, and the Roadrunner would always manage to escape or completely avoid it. However, Wylie was not that fortunate. He often got caught in his own trap. He'd set them up and set them off. When the dust from the explosion cleared, Wylie would be standing straight up, stiff as a board, and covered with dirt. It appeared that the explosion did not seriously damage him. He only seemed to be a little dirty and disheveled. But then the Roadrunner would come along, let out a couple of "beep beeps" and with a puff he would blow on Wylie. At that point the coyote would topple over making a loud thudding sound.

Many of you may have been in situations that have injured you. Like the coyote, outwardly there is very little evidence of the harm done to you. Outwardly you stand as a tower of strength. But the wound you carry is embedded in your heart. You try to make sense out of what happened, or why you. You delude yourself into thinking all is well and suddenly you are struck by a small dart and puff, just like Wylie Coyote you topple over. And still you try to hide your pain.

The issues that are causing you to hurt must be dealt with. Wherever *you* go, *you* will always be there. That is the difference between the ground and the field, even when you step out of the field, you will still be standing on ground—a battleground. There is no escaping; victory must be achieved where you stand. Taking a stance and facing a hurt is a hard decision. But it is time to stop running. You have been on an emotional treadmill long enough.

No one escapes a battle without being wounded or scarred in some way. *Staying there* has to do with defining your problem, facing your problem, opening yourself up to the Lord and allowing Him to apply healing balm to your heart. *Staying there* has to do with staying in a place of wholeness once you have been healed.

Many times we cloak our hurts in order to protect ourselves and give a false impression to others. The word that comes to mind is façade. The Lord gave me a sort of acronym for façade. A <u>fa</u>ce <u>a</u>rranged to <u>de</u>ceive. We feign arrogance or independence rather than let people see the real us. Rather than face the enemy within, we strike out at the ones closest to us. This kind of thing has led to division and discord among families and friends.

CHOOSE YOUR BATTLE

I have a friend who says, "Choose your battle." Although I like the phrase, I am not exactly sure what she means when she says it. I can only tell you what it means to me. From my point of view "choose your battle" means I will make a choice as to how I will take on a battle. For example if I have a drug problem, do I want to struggle with kicking the habit? Or do I continue to use drugs, risking jail time, losing my children, or perhaps even dying?

Using another example, as a child I was abused and for years I kept it buried, pretending it never happened. Do I allow the abuse to make me bitter? Or do I go through the pain of facing the truth? Facing the problem head on might necessitate confronting my abuser. This is what it may take in order for me to be healed. A woman or a man who enters into marriage with any unresolved issues of abuse is in danger of having a failed marriage. Choose your battle. The right decision may be the hardest to make. Even if your abuser is not around anymore you have access to the Lord, so your healing is still attainable.

Some years back on one of my daily walks, God spoke to me about wounds. I'd like to share the illustration. When a wound is inflicted it must be treated right away, even if it is only superficial.

In treating a wound you may apply a salve or an antibiotic before putting a bandage on it. However, the wound must not go unattended for too long a period. Occasionally, you have to remove the bandage, wash the infected area, and reapply salve. Depending on the severity of the wound, even the removal of the bandage can be painful. But in order to tend the wound the bandage must be removed. After a time, the wound is healed. The amount of time it takes for the injury to heal depends on the depth of the injury and the treatment applied.

In order to be healed you must choose to face the problem. Confronting your area of hurt is the beginning of the healing process. Even the slightest injury will begin to fester if left untreated. It is difficult to bring up subjects that can make the pain as fresh as if the offense just took place. But it must be done. A *one-time* conversation with your pastor or a close friend is not going to fix it, anymore than tending to a physical wound once will cause the wound to heal completely.

With the aid of prayer and quality time spent in counseling, you will eventually heal. So don't get discouraged. The bandage must be removed and the balm applied over and over before you begin to see any sign of healing.

A wound bleeds and a lion smells blood. The Bible equates Satan to a roaring lion. He is the lion and the hunter. He picks up the scent of your hurt and moves in for the kill. There is no scent of blood in a wound that has been healed. A scar will be the only evidence that an injury ever occurred.

A scar represents a memory of what once was. However, a scar no longer produces pain. A festering hurt will impair your ability to forgive. People (some Christians) have been known to say you should forgive and forget. It is a misconception to think you can blank an injustice done to you out of your mind. It may be subconsciously buried, but it still exists to resurface at any time. God commands you to forgive, but only He has the ability to forget a wrong.

Although a scar remains, the incident associated with it should not impede your ability to forgive. When you are able to forgive an injustice done to you, then you know you have truly been healed.

FEAR VERSUS FAITH

An all to common struggle that many face is the fear of dying. I am not speaking of the fear of death, but dying. Death is a loss of one's life, dying means to be on one's last leg, so to speak.

Although no one is anxious to die, most matured Christians are not terrified at the thought of death. According to my Bible, to be absent from the body is to be present with the Lord. However, most of us want to live well. I mean that in the sense of being whole. An emotional bondage will hinder you from living an abundant life.

This is how an emotional bondage works. Let's say you have lost a parent, a cousin, and a sibling to a debilitating disease. They all contracted the disease and died before the age of sixty-five and in three years you will be sixty-five. You began to live in fear because statistics tells you the disease is hereditary. Or maybe you allow superstition to rule your life. You figure the odds are two-to-one that what happened to them is going to happen to you. So instead of enjoying life, you live in dread wondering what the next day is going to bring. The irony is, an emotional bondage will not only strip you of your peace, but may make you physically ill.

According to Proverbs, *Anxiety in the heart of man causes depression, but a good word makes it glad (Proverbs 12:25).*

And, *A merry heart does good, like medicine, But a broken spirit dries the bones (Proverbs 17:22).*

86

Satan wants to steal your peace, but he cannot steal that which is guarded. Remember the word of God tells you; *Watch over your heart with all diligence, for from it flow the springs of life (Proverbs 4:23).*

Don't be put into bondage by what has happened to someone else. It may never happen to you. We must never discount the power of prayer. The answer to your healing is in knowing and trusting Jesus Christ. If you are not in a Bible study, get into one. Align yourself with brothers and sisters who know the word and will minister to you in moments when you are hurting and feeling vulnerable. Share your dark secret with a trusted friend. If you have not yet wept for yourself, it is time.

Remember *The Path* to intimacy. All is well in the presence of God. Stay on the path and the battle will truly be the Lord's. Because of His love for mankind, He works with regard to human life. He will bring peace in your spirit. He will cause joy to leap up in your soul. He will cause the spirit of fear to flee from you, because as you draw near to God He will draw near to you. And you will never again feel yourself in a battle alone. You have only to trust.

PRAYER: *God, I choose this day to be free from the bondage that has held me captive. I make a choice to forgive and I take hold of the freedom that comes with forgiveness. I release fear and embrace faith. I release unforgiveness and embrace healing. I thank you that all is well within me. Amen.*

THE PORTAL

Today is Thanksgiving Day and I want to wish you a Happy Thanksgiving. Even if you are not celebrating Thanksgiving as you read this, be thankful anyway. Everyday you are given is a gift from God and thanks is always in order. In the mornings when we open our eyes we should give God *Thanks* for *giving* us another *Day.*

There is a psalm of David that reads, *Stand in awe, and sin not: commune with your own heart upon your bed, and be still (Psalm 4:4).*

Upon waking up have you ever had an occasion to just lie in bed? In the quietness has God ever spoken to your heart?

I have come to realize when I awake in the morning, I am more sensitive to the voice of God then at any other time of the day. Of course, that may be because my days are filled with a variety of sounds. The sound may only be that of a Christian radio station, still, it is a voice other than God's. Christian programs are good to listen to, but we must never forget that God desires time with us and it is not always in the mornings. If you remember, earlier I stated that the principal theme of this book has to do with relational intimacy between you and God.

I have expressed the above as an introduction to *The Portal.*

It was on one of those mornings that I awoke with my mind on Jesus. There is a song we sing with a stanza that reads, "Woke up this morning with my mind stayed on Jesus." I often wonder how many live the songs they sing.

Although it was my intention to go back to sleep, the Lord was urging me to get up and pray. Being a typical human being I have a quirk or two. Maybe the word idiosyncrasy would best describe what I am about to reveal. When I get up in the morning, I must brush my teeth before I pray. I don't want to be in anyone's face with "morning breath," not even God's. Understand, when I pray I am whisked away and I find myself in the presence of the Almighty. Washing my face could wait until after prayer, but the breath had to be fresh. I trust you are not getting analytical; I've already admitted that it is one of my idiosyncrasies. You probably have one or two yourself.

After brushing my teeth I returned to my bedroom to pray. As I was praying the Lord spoke to me. He said, "Your home is to be a portal to my kingdom." At the time I did not understand what that meant or why God made that specific statement to me.

When I finished praying, I ran downstairs (before washing my face) to look up the word portal. Knowing God had said something deep and profound to me, I grabbed the encyclopedia for the letter *P* and looked for the word portal, it wasn't there. Then it came to me where I had heard the word many times before, it was on television, *Star Trek* to be exact.

Now I was beginning to question was it God who spoke. What a strange terminology for God to use.

The word portal was not to be found in any of my study books either. Finally I picked up the dictionary. There it was right between the words portague and portamento (in case you want to look it up). Webster said, "A portal is a doorway or an entrance, particularly one on a large scale."

Okay, I got that definition. But I knew I was still missing the full revelation of what God meant. I understood we were to tell everyone who came through our door about Jesus. That much was clear. What else did God want from us?

CAN GOD GET A WITNESS?

Over the past five years we have had quite a bit of work done on our house and quite a few people coming through. We witnessed to some, but not to all. At the present we are having a bathroom built in our basement. My husband had already talked to our contractor about Jesus. I told him what God said. This opened our eyes even more concerning the responsibility and the importance of telling *all* who came through our doors about Jesus.

Little by little I was given more insight on the portal. Not only was our structural home to be a place of witnessing, but also wherever we went we were to tell about Jesus. Because we are born again believers, our bodies house the Holy Spirit.

The Living Bible puts it like this, *Haven't you yet learned that your body is the home of the Holy Spirit God gave you, and that he lives within you? (1 Corinthians 6:19)*

When God said to me, "Make your home a portal to my kingdom," He was merely reminding me of the charge He has given to every Christian.

The first four letters in the word portal spell "port." One definition of port means to carry in a military fashion. Although Satan is a strategic enemy, he is also a defeated foe. We are to be militant in our faith because we are in the army of God. We are His prayer warriors. We should be skilled in the word of God, using it to attack the demonic forces which have captured our children, invaded our churches, come against our marriages, and enticed us to compromise.

I want to bring to mind a certain Bible story found in the book of Acts.

Some Jews who went around driving out evil spirits tried to invoke the name of the Lord Jesus over those who were demon-possessed. They would say, "In the name of Jesus, whom Paul preaches, I command you to come out."

Seven sons of Sceva, a Jewish chief priest, were doing this. [One day] the evil spirit answered them, "Jesus I know, and I know about Paul, but who are you?" Then the man who had the evil spirit jumped on them and overpowered them all. He gave them such a beating that they ran out of the house naked and bleeding.

When the Jews and Greeks living in Ephesus knew this, they were all seized with fear, and the name of the Lord Jesus was held in high honor (Acts 19:13-17).

In other words, because Jesus was magnified, the people who believed that *He* was who *He* said He was came forward and confessed their sins.

Jesus was a portal to the kingdom of God. Paul was a portal to the kingdom of God. Christian, if you personify the one you claim to serve, you too will be a portal to the kingdom of God.

For though we walk in the flesh, we do not war according to the flesh. For the weapons of our warfare are not carnal but mighty in God for pulling down strongholds (2 Corinthians 10:3,4).

Keep in mind that Satan is forever seeking out those who are without the full armor of God. He looks for those who are unaware and uneducated in the word of God. It takes staying power to be victorious. Staying in the word, staying in a posture of prayer, and staying vigilant.

Jesus said, *I am the way, the truth, and the life. No one comes to the Father except through me (John 14: 6).*

Jesus is the portal to the kingdom of His Father. He was and still is our example. He taught people about the kingdom; He died so that we would have access to it. You may say, "I am not going to die for anyone, especially those who don't appreciate me. They don't deserve kindness because they are not kind. They are rotten and will never amount to anything. If I am going to give my life, at least it will be for someone who cares about me."

Is this our attitude?

Yet Jesus tells us that we are supposed to die daily. We are to die to our selfish ways. We are to deny ourselves. We are to deny pride and not be ashamed to share the gospel. We are to deny flesh and live a life of obedience. We are to deny our priorities for material things and be willing to share with others, even strangers and those who have treated us spitefully—remember Jesus—our door to the kingdom.

Even those of us who envision ourselves as portals may have such narrow openings (are of such narrow minds) people are afraid to attempt entry. I'm referring to the manner in which the gospel must be shared. We must be very careful when sharing the good news as it relates to Jesus. It should be done with a loving spirit and not a critical one. When we share from the depths of our hearts we are more approachable. We widen the doorway and make entry into the kingdom more desirable (and accessible).

Often when people see us on fire for the Lord, they may not be able to relate to us as ever having been a gambler, a liar, a drug addict, a back stabber, a lover of alcohol. Or whatever sin had us in its ugly clutches. The point being, share openly and honestly because there are those who believe they are too evil to be saved or worse— loved by God. According to their way of thinking they must do some form of penance in order to be saved. They find it difficult to accept as truth all that's required is to repent from their old way of thinking and believe on the Lord Jesus Christ. They must also realize the belief *should* be accompanied by a change in their lifestyle.

JUST LIKE JESUS

There's a woman who would habitually call me. She was always going through something. Each time she called I tried to comfort her. In an effort to relate to some of her situations, I would share things about myself. She never seemed to be listening; she seemed only interested in having me as a guest at her party—her pity party.

Although I found this to be very exasperating, I endeavored to help her whenever she called. I would try to find a Scripture that addressed her problem. After subjecting myself to many a depressing conversation, she turned on me.

One day out of the blue she called me up and confronted me with all sorts of lies. Immediately my blood began to boil. I thought of all the times I talked with her when I didn't feel like being bothered. I thought about all the depressing conversations I had endured and I was sorry I had ever tried to help her. Ever felt that way about anyone?

There are no intelligent or civilized words to describe the anger and disgust I felt for her at that moment. I did not want to act like a godly woman in any fashion whatsoever. I just wanted her to finish with what she had to say so I could chew her up and spit her out. I knew I had the ability to do it, too. I was a much *stronger* woman than she was. I knew I was out of control and I didn't care. I was going to feel much better as soon as I told her a thing or two.

Finally she stopped talking and I was ready. But something happened. Before I could open my mouth to speak, Jesus spoke. What He said was of such magnitude, the rage within me miraculously left (as angry as I was it had to be a miracle). I don't know if it was the statement itself or the simple fact that it came from Jesus, but I'll never forget it.

In my spirit I heard these words, "I have presented you with an opportunity to be more like me."

Wow! What a pleasure. What a privilege. Jesus wanted me to emulate Him. We become angry or annoyed when folks mimic what we do. We don't want that sister in Christ to have a pretty suit identical to our pretty suit or that brother to fix up his yard to look just like our yard, but Jesus—wanted me—to imitate Him.

I calmed her down and tried to get to the root of the problem. I had to deny pride, I had to deny anger, and at that moment I had to bear a cross for that woman. It was not the time to stand in judgment. She was in pain and she needed to be comforted. She needed for me to be kinder to her than I had ever been in the past.

In the book of Luke it says, *Judge not, and you will not be judged; condemn not, and you will not be condemned; forgive, and you will be forgiven; give, and it will be given to you; good measure, pressed down, shaken together, running over, will be put into your lap. For the measure you give will be the measure you get back (Luke 6:37,38).*

Often, I've heard this scripture preached when it came to giving an offering of money. But not when it came to sacrificing the things in one's flesh that displease God. If I had retaliated I would not have been a portal. I would have been a closed door. To date she still calls me. She is growing but, like most of us regardless of where we are, still has a long way to go.

Today I challenge you to "make your house a portal to the kingdom of God."

PRAYER: *My Lord and my God, too many times I have ignored the urging of your Spirit. Forgive me for those times I have failed to share your plan of salvation. Forgive me for judging when I should have been more loving. I pray today that I will be instrumental in leading someone to you. Help me not to fail the person who will need my help. Give me the words to say as I pray for them. In Jesus' name I thank you. Amen.*

THE STORM

Then they cry out to the LORD in their trouble, And He brings them out of their distresses. He calms the storm, so that its waves are still. Then they are glad because they are quiet; So He guides them to their desired haven. Oh, that man would give thanks to the LORD for His goodness (Psalm 107:28-31).

A storm is a violent disturbance that comes upon you suddenly. Whether it is a snowstorm, a rainstorm, or a hailstorm, the sun may be shining brightly one moment and the next moment you find yourself in a storm.

I have an adult daughter. As a child she was very precocious. I knew before she was born that this child was going to keep me on my toes. When I was pregnant with her she was very still as long as I was up and moving about. On the other hand, the moment I'd lay down, no matter what time of day, she would kick me. Her little foot, or fist, would strike so hard you could see the imprint on my stomach each time it shot forth. She would not simply kick and retract; she'd hold that little foot out as if she were trying to push me into an upright position. She'd push out and I'd place my hands on my stomach in an effort to push her little foot back where it belonged. It was then I realized it was going to be a "war of the wills" between this bundle of joy and me. I could tell you of a number of episodes concerning my daughter, which would prove I was right in my perceptions. However, I'm going to skip all that and tell you about a statement she made when she was a young child.

When Tracie was barely eight, she and I lived in a very fashionable apartment complex. The surroundings were quiet. We had all sorts of security. There were cameras and intercoms, as well as guards who patrolled the grounds. Therefore, I felt as if I had provided a safe living environment for her. Our life was average. She went to school and I worked. When I came home I would fix something for the two of us to eat. The rest of the evening we lounged around the apartment until bedtime. That was our routine during the week.

After dinner we were accustomed to having dessert, usually it was ice cream. One day, in the midst of preparing dinner I realized we didn't have anything for dessert. Being creatures of habit, not to mention having a love for ice cream, I turned the stove off and told my daughter I was going to run out to the store and get some ice cream. I assured her that it would not take me long and I would be right back. After all, the store was less than ten minutes away.

While I was in the kitchen preparing dinner, my daughter was in the living room watching television. It was summertime, so although it was around 6:30 in the evening, the sun was shining brightly. Unbeknownst to me, a storm warning had been broadcast during a station break. So when I announced to my daughter that I was going to the store, she looked up at me with an expression of horror.

She said, "Mommy, I'm scared to be here by myself, there's going to be a storm."

I took a quick look out of the balcony window.

I turned to my daughter and said, "No it's not, honey, see how bright the sun is shining."

This took place in the summer of 1975, and what she said next is something that has always stuck with me.

My daughter looked me in the eyes and in a very serious manner, with much insight she said, "Don't nobody know what God's going to do."

She was so right. I could argue all day about the inaccuracies of the weather reports, but I had no defense against that statement. It so happened that my grandmother lived in the same building on the same floor, so I took Tracie around to her apartment while I ran to the store and bought the ice cream.

The storms in our lives can spring up just as suddenly as a weather storm. One minute your life will be bright and rosy and the next minute it's overcast. God may send sunshine to chase away the storm or he may send a storm that obstructs the sunshine.

As quick as a flash of lightening, a stroke can debilitate you, the loss of a job may financially cripple you, the passing of a loved one throws you into a panic, a fire destroys everything you own, or a child is taken from you. The thunder claps and in an instant your health, your wealth, and your sense of well-being are snatched away. You find yourself trying to hold on for dear life while the tempest rages all around you. There is no way to know when God is going to allow a storm to come into your life. And there is no way to know when or how He will deliver you from it. What you should keep in mind is that He said He would never leave you or forsake you. Remember the story of Job.

As violent as a storm can be, you can weather it if you have something secure to hold onto. If you can grasp that which is constant, you will not be destroyed by the storm. God and His word are constant. If you put your trust in Him, there is no need to know what God is going to do next in your life. Trusting and knowing Him should dispel all of your fears. To know God means to have an intimate relationship with Him. When you have intimacy with God you will trust Him to do what is best, because you know His character. And you believe the love He has for you.

A FIRM FOUNDATION

The Psalmist says, *My heart is fixed, O God, my heart is fixed: I will sing and give praise (Psalm 57:7).*

This was written during a period when David was running for his life. King Saul wanted to kill him. There was a time when David was living in the palace of the king, eating at the king's table, and in charge of the king's army. He married one of the king's daughters. Now he found himself running for his life, hiding in caves, often hungry, and sometimes afraid. Being married to the king's daughter had not offered him any security. Being over the king's army did not ensure his protection. Sitting at King Saul's table was not a guarantee that he would never go hungry. At the time this verse was written, David found himself in a storm.

Yet he said, "My heart is fixed."

Other translations of the Bible use the words "quiet," "content," and "steadfast" in place of the word fixed.

Twice the Psalmist conveys, "My heart is fixed."

And just so there is no doubt as to whom David is speaking, the second time he says, *O God my heart is fixed.*

Again he says, *God, my heart is fixed; I will sing and give praise, even with my glory (Psalm 108:1).*

Tell us that the righteous man shall not be afraid of an evil report: his heart should be fixed, trusting in the LORD (Psalm 112:7).

David had no idea how God was going to move next, but he trusted Him because he knew His character. In the midst of the storm, he stood firm. His faith in God was unshakable. David knew God to be forever steadfast.

What do you grab hold of when the storms are raging in your life? If you want to come out of the storm still standing, you'll have to take hold of that which is found to be stable, constant, and established. Is alcohol your answer in the storm? That will only cause you to reel more. Is hiding your answer? That will only cause you to be caught off guard. Is staying home from church what you do when the storm comes? That will only isolate you from the people who may be able to help you through it.

The roots of a tree go deep into the earth. In order for a tree to be destroyed in a storm it must be rotten or pulled up by the roots. The depth of the roots determines the strength of the tree. Deep roots secure the tree.

The Living Bible puts it like this, *But blessed is the man who trusts in the Lord and has made the Lord his hope and confidence. He is like a tree planted along a riverbank, with its roots reaching deep into the water, a tree not bothered by the heat nor worried by long months of drought. Its leaves stay green, and it goes right on producing all its luscious fruit (Jeremiah 17:7,8).*

God wants you to be unshakable in your faith. He doesn't want your heart to be fearful.

That's why He said through his servant Paul, *Be anxious for nothing, but in everything by prayer and supplication, with thanksgiving, let your requests be made known to God; and the peace of God, which surpasses all understanding, will guard your hearts and minds through Christ Jesus (Philippians 4:6,7).*

The instinctive thing to do when caught in a storm is run for shelter.

For You have been a shelter for me, A strong tower from the enemy. I will abide in Your tabernacle forever; I will trust in the shelter of Your wings (Psalm 61:3,4).

A shelter is a haven in a storm. Use your time of "going through" as a time of reflection. You may need to set new priorities, especially if you come to realize you only call on God when times are bad. Consider that even in your storm, you can be a blessing to someone. Remember after the storm comes the rainbow.

I would like to end this story with a beautiful analogy that came across my desk. I don't know the author; it was signed anonymous. However, it blessed my soul. I hope it does the same for you.

A little girl walked to and from her elementary school. One morning it was particularly cloudy as she made her daily trek. As the afternoon progressed the winds whipped up. The air roared with thunder and flashes of lightning streaked across the sky. The mother of the little girl was concerned that her daughter would be frightened as she walked home in the storm. She herself feared that the electrical storm might harm her child.

Full of concern and anxiety, the mother quickly got into her car and drove along the route to her child's school. As she did so she saw her little girl walking along, but with each flash of lightning the child would stop, look up and smile. Flash after flash would quickly follow and with each, the child would look up at the streak of light and smile.

The mother drove her car up alongside her daughter, she lowered the window and called to her, "What are you doing? Why do you keep stopping?" *The child smiled and answered, "I'm trying to look pretty. God keeps taking my picture."*

The mother saw the storm as a threat. The child saw God in the storm and she saw Him being especially attentive to her. May God bless you today as you face the storms that come your way.

PRAYER: *Father God, give me the strength to give thanks in spite of the storm. Help me not to turn my face from you. Please calm me in the midst of the storm. I know if I trust you I will make it through. Forgive me for complaining when I should have been praying. In my weakness, guide me to those who will put me in remembrance of your word. Thank you, Father. Amen.*

ADDENDUM

A MESSAGE FROM THE AUTHOR

THE COLORS OF CHRISTMAS

~~~~~~

Christmas is one of my favorite times of the year. It has nothing to do with gift giving, though I like receiving gifts as well as the next person. But if I never received one gift, it would still be one of my favorite times.

I hear you asking, "What makes it special to me?"

I love the colors that represent Christmas.

Some years ago when the Lord spoke to me about the colors we see during the yuletide season, I was quite excited. Until that time, I had never thought of them as being applicable to a Christian's life. I had never before related the red, green, gold, and white display of ornaments, trees, lights, and decorations to anything other than the traditions of the holiday. However, recently I've heard that these colors were not to be used as Christmas decorations in one of the area establishments—which I will leave unnamed.

That started me thinking, there must be something to these colors. So as an addendum to my book, I thought I might share the colors of Christmas with you.

I hope that the next few statements don't offend anyone. Of course, I know there are some who look for offense. I am not overly concerned about those types. I just hope you see the point of truth.

After September 11, 2001 (the date of the terrorist bombings of the Twin Towers in New York City, and the Pentagon in Washington, D.C.) the colors of many outdoor Christmas lights were red, white, and blue. These are the proud colors of our flag, and I myself am proud to be an American. I am proud of the things our flag is meant to stand for.

Many red, white, and blue lights were arranged in the shape of our flag. There were displays of red, white, and blue lights that read "God bless America." Christmas trees were adorned with red, white, and blue lights. As Americans we were not ashamed to let anyone know where we stood and what we stood for.

It was not merely the flag itself; it was the colors of the flag. The red, white, and blue represented our patriotism to America. If it were just about the flag the declaration of red, white, and blue Christmas lights would not have symbolized anything. If it were just about the flag, any color lights would have done. No, it was about the colors red, white, and blue, which denote our flag. They speak loudly about our allegiance to our country. Granted, there are other countries that bear the same colors. But what do you think of when you hear the term "Old Glory" or "The Stars and Stripes?" You think of the colors red, white, and blue.

In 1782, the Congress of Confederation gave a meaning to these colors. Red stood for hardiness and courage; white for purity and innocence; and blue stood for vigilance, perseverance, and justice.

I hope I have brought to your attention the fact that colors do mean something to us. I want to parallel our allegiance to our country to a Christian's allegiance to God. To do so I am going to use the colors red, green, gold, and white—the colors of Christmas.

The last time I checked, we were a Christian nation, although we are incognito. Prayer is no longer allowed in school. There have been movements to remove God's name off buildings and out of courtrooms. Many public places no longer allow the Nativity scene to be put on display at Christmastime. Diversity has replaced unity.

Still we identify ourselves as a Christian nation when it is convenient to do so. What has happened to one nation under God?

Now what about the colors we normally see at Christmastime? There is **red,** the color of blood. Jesus said, *For this is my blood of the New Testament, which is shed for many for the remission of sins (Matthew 26:28).*

Blood is the river of life. To achieve salvation for man, Jesus permitted life to flow out of Him. He gave His life so that every living soul could attain freedom. His blood gives us freedom from psychological bondage and eternal death.

Next there's **green**, the color of a healthy thriving life. Psalm 1:3 says, *The righteous should be like trees planted by the rivers of water, that brings forth its fruit in its season, whose leaf also shall not wither; And whatever he* [the righteous man] *does shall prosper.*

The Bible tells us we are to grow in grace and in the knowledge of our Lord and Savior. When we see a plant that is green we know it is

115

growing, but when we see a brown plant which is suppose to be green we know it is dead or dying.

When I see the color green I think of growth. I reflect on my own growth as a Christian. I ponder on such scriptures as, *The righteous shall flourish like the palm tree: he shall grow like a cedar in Lebanon (Psalm 92:12).*

Then there's the color white. I believe everyone thinks of good when they see white. You have white angel food cake in contrast to chocolate devils' food cake. The good cowboy wears the white hat and rides the white horse. While the bad cowboy wears the black hat and rides the black horse (with the exception of Zorro, it used to work that way).

As a Christian the color white reminds me of holiness, which is only one of God's many attributes.

There is no one holy like the LORD, Indeed, there is no one besides You, nor is there any rock like our God (1 Samuel 2:2).

Christmas is the time of year that has been set aside to celebrate the birth of the Son of God. I believe most Christians realize that we do not know the day Jesus was born nevertheless in honor of Him we celebrate His birth.

Because of the birth, crucifixion, burial, and resurrection of Jesus, under the new covenant we have the capability to be holy. If this were not true, God would not have commanded us to be so.

But as He who called you is holy, you also be holy in all your conduct, because it is written, Be holy, for I am holy (1 Peter 1:15,16).

We reflect on that which is seemingly without fault. Therefore many do not understand this verse. Being holy has been mistaken to mean perfection, although I could do a Bible study on the difference that is not my goal—right now. I suggest you do a Bible study if you are unsure about the difference.

It is the indwelling Holy Spirit that helps us to live holy lives. The color white reminds me of the virtuous lifestyle God expects us to demonstrate.

Last but not least we have the color **gold.** What comes to mind when you think of gold? Is it treasures or prosperity, or is having gold the solution to fulfillment?

The color gold makes me think of wealth and royalty. As a young child Jesus was presented with gifts of gold in celebration of His birth. The celebration we call Christmas.

After coming into the house they saw the Child with Mary His mother; and they fell to the ground and worshiped Him. Then, opening their treasures, they presented to Him gifts of gold, frankincense, and myrrh (Matthew 2:11).

These were gifts fit for a king. They had a meaning beyond what we read on the surface.

The frankincense was an aromatic used in sacrificial offerings. The myrrh perfumed the ointments used for burials, and was

117

emblematic of the sufferings Jesus would endure. The gold was presented to the infant King as a token of His royalty.

The prophetic, priestly, and kingly offices of Christ are to be seen in these gifts. He has fulfilled His prophetic office: the myrrh. He has filled His priestly office: the frankincense. Christians know Him today to be King of Kings: the gold.

The colors of our American flag representing courage, purity, justice and perseverance are all good. But let's not negate the colors of Christmas. Red representing our liberty through Christ; green signifying our daily growth in Him; white being symbolic of a holy lifestyle; and gold denoting our royal priesthood because we are reborn into royalty.

As we focus on America let us look to God. As we count the strengths of America, let us recognize the power behind the strength. As we shout "God bless America" let us bless the God of America. As we carry the flag with our hands, may we honor the Lord in our hearts. I hope you will look forward to the colors of Christmas.

AUTHOR'S CLOSING PRAYER

Father,

I have completed my assignment. I have asked your blessing on all who read this book. I pray each life has been transformed to your will. I pray that the reader of this book has a hunger for the miraculous. Not so they will be glorified, Father, but so you will be. Your people need to know that you still bring into being signs and wonders.

I thank you for the lives that have been changed. I thank you for the people who have been encouraged. I thank you for the relationships that have been healed. I thank you for your blessing on those who have fallen deeper in love with you. Most of all I thank you for the courage it took for me to write this book.

Lord, for those who will be caught in the Tribulation, I pray this book will give them the strength they need to make it through. But I pray mostly that they will be saved so they will not have to go through the struggle. Always, in Jesus' name.

Love,
Cheryl

REFERENCES

PC BIBLE STUDY - NEW KING JAMES, KING JAMES, NEW AMERICAN STANDARD—UPDATED EDITION, THE LIVING BIBLE, REVISED STANDARD VERSION
(Bible software—electronic database) Copyright 1999

THE INTERPRETER'S DICTIONARY of the **BIBLE**
(Abingdon Press – 13th printing) Copyright 1996

WORLD BOOK ENCYCLOPEDIA
(World Book, Inc.—Chicago, London, Sydney, Toronto) Copyright 1994

NOAH WEBSTER, WEBSTER'S TWENTIETH- CENTURY DICTIONARY OF ENGLISH LANGUAGE—UNABRIDGED LL.D., Edited by Thomas H. Russell, LL.D.; A.C. Bean, M.E., LL.B.; L.B. Vaughan, Ph. B (Publisher's Guild, Inc—New York, New York) Copyright 1936

ROBERT JAMIESON, A.R. FAUSSET, DAVID BROWN, JAMIESON, FAUSSET and BROWN COMMENTARY (electronic database by Biblesoft) Copyright 1997

SCRIPTURE INDEX

THE WATERFALL
Psalm 14:2
Luke 18:1
1 Thessalonians 5:17
1 Kings 17:2-10
1 Kings 17:17-24
Acts 10:38
Philippians 4:8

THE WILDERNESS
Luke 4:1
1 Corinthians 2:7, 8
1 Corinthians 7:10-14
Matthew 5:6
James 1:2-8
Luke 5:16

THE RAINBOW
Ecclesiastes 3:4
Genesis 9:11-14
Isaiah 58: 8, 9
Ezekiel 1:28
2 Corinthians 10:3-5
Ezekiel 28:13-16
Isaiah 14:12-14
John 10:10
Isaiah 42:16

THE PATH
Psalm 16:1
Psalm 37:4, 5
John 14: 27
Proverbs 2:7
2 Corinthians 5:7
John 15:9-12

THE STAR
Genesis 1:16-18
Psalm 147: 4, 5
Genesis 2:16,17
Genesis 3:6
Daniel 12:3, 4
1 Corinthians 10:13
John 8:59
Luke 22:42
1 Corinthians 5:20
Romans 8:17
1 Peter 2:9
Matthew 5:16

THE BRIDGE
Romans 8:28
1 Corinthians 15:3-6
Psalm 105:1-5

THE BATTLEGROUND
2 Corinthians 4:8, 9
Jeremiah 8:22
James 5:13,14
Luke 9:11
Proverbs 12:25
Proverbs 17:22
Proverbs 4:23

THE PORTAL
Psalm 4:4
1 Corinthians 6:19
Acts 19:13-17
2 Corinthians 10:3, 4
John 14:6
Luke 6:37, 38

THE STORM
Psalm 107:28-31
Psalm 57:7
Psalm 108:1
Psalm 112:7
Jeremiah 17:7,8
Philippians 4:6, 7
Psalm 61:3, 4

ADDENDUM
Matthew 26:28
Psalm 1:3
Psalm 92:12
1 Samuel 2:2
1 Peter 1:15,16
Matthew 2:11

ABOUT THE AUTHOR

Cheryl L. Wakes is a native of Cleveland, Ohio. She is a Bible study teacher, intercessor, workshop presenter, and speaker who loves the Lord. Although this is her first published book, writing is not new to her. She has written numerous poems and several of her writings have appeared in newsletters. She was inspired to write *Staying There* because of what she saw in the lives of many Christians... defeat. Her prayer is that *Staying There* will encourage strengthen and enrich the reader.

Cheryl believes when you pray, God gives you clarity. He has clearly given her something for each reader.

I f you wish to correspond with the author you may write or call her at:

12811 Speedway Overlook
E. Cleveland, Ohio 44112
(216) 451-4020

To God be the glory

Printed in the United States
20051LVS00007B/310-384